IRAQ

In the Crosshairs of Destiny

What the Bible Says About the Future of Iraq

Rev. 1:5-8

SOLA SCRIPTURA

*A*dvantage™
INSPIRATIONAL

Dan Hayden

Dedication

To my trusted friend and companion in ministry,

SCOTT PIERRE
Executive Director of Sola Scriptura,

with a deep sense of gratitude
for your constant encouragement
and support of this project.

Dan Hayden

Table of Contents

Acknowledgments

I offer my heartfelt appreciation to numerous individuals who have contributed to this project:

First and foremost – to Karilee my loving wife and most capable associate, encourager, valued consultant, diligent researcher, manuscript word processor and editing whiz. As always, this project is a combination of our efforts. Thanks for your many hours of hard work. In my love for you, I am truly thankful to God for your partnership in life.

To the Sola Scriptura staff Dean, Karen, Stu, Robert and Beth—who in so many ways have blessed my life as we work together in the pursuit of our ministry.

To my faithful and devoted A.C.T.S. class in the adult education program at First Baptist Church of Orlando, who first endured my teaching on this subject – "From Babylon to Baghdad," and who enthusiastically encouraged me to write this book.

To Les Stobbe – my literary agent. You are a true blessing to my life and ministry. Thank you for your tireless efforts on my behalf.

To Mike and Karyn Janiczek – creative publishers - for devoting the resources of Advantage Books to make this book a reality. Your enthusiasm for Christ and for this project has been a great encouragement to me.

To Dana Parker – editor, for giving this work your most careful attention; and for your insights, revisions and suggestions that have made this book better than it would have been.

To each I express my most humble and sincere thanks.

Dan Hayden

IN GOD'S TIME

Iraq is a nation in conflict. But then, Iraq always has been a region immersed in conflict. The history of Iraq is a sad story of foreign intrusion and the rule of others.

Beginning with such promise (the Babylonian Empire of Hammurabi in the third millennium BC and Nebuchadnezzar's Neo-Babylonian Empire from 612 to 539 BC), the land known as Mesopotamia quickly lost its status among the nations and never recovered.

Until the early years of the twentieth century AD, the people of the area could only dream of national sovereignty, let alone the possibility of greatness in the world. In one generation, however, Saddam Hussein changed all that.

As a country, Iraq has only recently been known as "Iraq." Officially the area had been known as Mesopotamia, the land between the rivers. Iraq, however, is an ancient Aramaic word meaning "black, muddy land."[1] Arabs have been referring to the region as "Iraq" since the middle ages, but only since World War I has there been a country by that name.

Black mud simply described the fertile nature of the land along the Tigris and Euphrates rivers. Black meant that the land possessed rich agricultural soil and it was muddy because of sufficient water in an otherwise arid, inhospitable part of the world. To be known as a black, muddy land in the Middle East was to be called a prince among paupers.

If Egypt was the gift of the Nile, as Herodotus once said, then Iraq was doubly blessed as the gift of the Tigris and Euphrates.

So, how did Iraq decline from black, muddy soil to brown, dry sand? And what factors led to the emergence of this seemingly nowhere place into international prominence?

Oil is part of the picture, of course, but that's not the whole story. In fact, oil is only a contributing factor in a much broader scheme. Physically, Iraq is mostly brown sand rather than black mud due to centuries of neglect. Nationally, however, Iraq has emerged out of the mud and sand to become a prominent player in world affairs because God has determined that it should be so. That is the message of the Bible.

IRAQ'S IMPROBABLE RISE TO PROMINENCE

Consider for a moment some of the improbabilities in this momentous ascendancy of a minor nation to world obsession.

Geographic Impediments

First of all, Iraq is not prestigious geographically. It is a relatively small country—a mere 168,000 square miles, making it slightly larger than the state of California. About 650 miles in length (the distance from Miami to Atlanta), Iraq varies in width from 480 miles in the central portion of the country to 25 miles in the south.

The land along the rivers is agricultural, but most of the extended portions of the territory are inhospitable desert. Most of the 43 million inhabitants live in the urban areas sprinkled along the shores of the two rivers. By way of contrast, California boasts a population of 36 million.

Ethnic Challenges

Secondly, Iraq is ethnically diverse. 85% of its population is Arab, but an unhealthy racial mix of Kurds in the north and Iranians (and Iranian loyalists) in the south has resulted in a coexistence nightmare. The Kurds (the largest minority group) descend from the ancient Medes, while the Iranians are Persians. The two groups have a long history of conflict, in both ancient Babylon and modern Iraq. A coalition of Medes and Persians were the spoilers of the Neo-Babylonian Empire of the sixth century BC, which explains Saddam Hussein's hatred for both of them. He wanted to subjugate them, even punish them, for their past hostilities. Genocide with biological weapons of mass destruction was no ethical problem to Saddam. In his mind, it was deserved.

Religious Conflict

Thirdly, 90% of Iraq is Muslim, but that does not mean that Muslim solidarity exists. A stringent division separates them. **Shi'as** (or purists) are the largest group, with strong ties to Iran. These are essentially the Muslims of the southern districts which have spawned the majority of radical Islamic terrorists after the Iraqi Freedom War. Yet, the minority **Sunnis**—the traditionalists—have been the ruling power for most of Iraq's short history. Now, however, they find themselves on the short end of the new representative government, and much of the insurgent violence plaguing the country is to the Sunnis' discredit.

Saddam professed allegiance to the Sunni tradition, but appeared to be more committed to the pan-Arabism of his Ba'ath political party. Having and exercising despotic authority was evidently more important to him than the will of Allah. The point I'm making is that the Shi'as and the Sunnis are competing factions—antagonists in the struggle for power. Their preferred means of settling differences historically has been violence, not negotiation.

Add to this the factious politics of colonialism, nationalism, communism, and a host of other "isms"—and the scenario of disunity and chaos emerges. No wonder the coalition forces of the Iraqi Freedom War are struggling in the formation of a representative government for the future of Iraq. These people don't like each other.

In the tradition of Ali Baba and his Forty Thieves, these contrary factions would rather slit each other's throats than talk about getting along. And yet the impossible appears to be happening. Why?

Financial Peril

Before I seek to answer that question (in the first chapter of this book), let me raise a fourth observation. Were it not for the scamming that took place with the U.N. Oil for Food program, Saddam's Iraq was on the verge of bankruptcy. Deeply in debt due to its decade-long war with Iran, Iraq was facing economic disaster. Saddam's invasion of Kuwait seemed to be more out of desperation than a calculated move of expansionism. He needed their oil and their money. Otherwise, Iraq apparently was headed for the scrapheap of obsolete nations.

WHAT'S HAPPENING TODAY IN IRAQ?

So, what's the deal? What we're seeing today shouldn't be happening. Why then is it happening?

Quite simply, it appears that the time has come and God's plan is in motion. Saddam Hussein's rise to power, elusive weapons of mass destruction, two international wars in the desert, and a U.S. imposed struggle for democracy are all merely details in the biblical anticipation for this land as history rushes from Babylon to Baghdad—and back to Babylon.

This book looks at that prophetic history. It is God's plan for Iraq as unfolded in the Bible. It is also a peek at things to come.

PART ONE

UNRAVELING THE MYSTERY

Dan Hayden

Chapter One

OUT OF THE MUD
Iraq's Emergence into World Prominence

So, what's your ultimate fear? What makes your skin crawl, sends shivers up your spine, and causes your heart play irregular rhythms like a bongo drum on speed?

For some people, it's spiders. Arachnophobia, the fear of spiders, instills an uncontrollable urge either to run and hide or to squash and annihilate the eight-legged monsters. "They are creepy and fearsome, and some of them can actually kill you," my phobic friend insists. "The world would really be better off without them!"

Well, there's now an "Iraqnophobia" in the land that is every bit as disquieting.

Iraq is a strange, far-away country, and it's killing a lot of people. Half of America, according to recent polls, wants the U.S. to abandon the scene. Most people realize that all Iraqis are not terrorists, but there are enough of the lethal variety to raise the hackles on the phobic's neck. "Stay away from Iraq. It's filled with two-legged Iraq-noids and you might end up dead," they warn. "When it comes to Islamic fundamentalists," they add, "the world would be better off without them."

Like orcs emerging out of the slime of Saruman's incubation pits in *The Lord of the Rings*, Iraqi terrorists have risen out of the mud and sand of Mesopotamia to become the nemesis of America. What is it, then, about this strange place snuggled amongst the more notable regimes of Jordan, Syria, Turkey, Iran, and Saudi Arabia that it should be awarded such a prominent position in the international affairs of the twenty-first century?

Well, terrorism and oil, for openers. But is that all? Could there be more here than meets the eye? Are we in fact witnessing the emergence of a divinely orchestrated pageant of epic proportions? It is my opinion that this is exactly what we are seeing.

For our first clue, let's go back to the beginning when Iraq, then known as Babylon, towered above the nations of the Middle East.

WISDOM FROM IRAQ

Would it surprise you to learn that the wisest man in ancient Iraq was a Jew from Israel? I'm not kidding. Given Iraq's hatred for the Jews, this is indeed big news. And, it's true. His name was Daniel, and there is a book in the Hebrew Scriptures named after him. Actually, he wrote it.

When the great king of Babylon, Nebuchadnezzar, conquered Israel in 605 BC, he deposed Israel's monarchy and took a group of young Israelis from the royal family back to Babylon with him. You see, Babylon had a policy of taking young potential leaders from a conquered country for the purpose of retraining them as Babylonians. The more gifted among them were then given opportunities to serve in the government of Nebuchadnezzar. That's how a smart Jewish kid from Jerusalem ended up working in the political system of Babylon.

Now Daniel was not only the valedictorian of his Babylonian class, he also stood out as being unusually gifted as an interpreter of dreams and a predictor of future events. In fact, it wasn't long before he was appointed by Nebuchadnezzar himself to the highest position among the king's counselors. As chief of the Babylonian Magi, or wise men, Daniel's reputation became legendary.

In the second chapter of the Book of Daniel, the beginning of the fascinating story of Daniel's meteoric rise to national prominence is recorded. It's a bizarre account of political intrigue that could only happen in Iraq. In this story, Daniel's involvement was actually crucial to the survival of the entire caste of Magi.

Nebuchadnezzar was a self-centered tyrant. Sound familiar? As the supreme ruler of the Neo-Babylonian Empire, he exercised despotic power. On this occasion Daniel discovered Nebuchadnezzar's whimsical and sadistic notion to exterminate the entire cadre of scholarly leadership in his kingdom simply because they could not interpret one of his bad dreams—without his even telling them what the dream was.[1] Nebuchadnezzar was subject to no law but himself. That is why Daniel quoted God as saying that he was a "king of kings"[2]—because he enjoyed an absolute power that other kings could only imagine.

In this initial portion of the story, Daniel pled the case for Babylon's wise men and disaster was averted. In private prayer with his God, Daniel expressed the conviction of his soul before making a request for divine disclosure of the king's dream: "Blessed be the name of God forever and ever . . . he removes kings and sets up kings . . ."[3]

You see, Daniel knew who was in control, and it wasn't Nebuchadnezzar.

Later, as Daniel exposed the dream and its interpretation to the king, that conviction of divine sovereignty spoken in private prayer became a public disclosure of the king's legitimacy. Looking Nebuchadnezzar in the eye with the intensity of an angelic pronouncement, Daniel leveled the king to a common player beneath the sovereign hand of God. "You, O king, the king of kings, to whom the God of heaven has given the kingdom, the power, and the might, and the glory . . . "[4] In one stroke of the tongue, Nebuchadnezzar was reduced from a proud monarch with absolute authority to a simple man to whom God had been generous.

The Neo-Babylonian Empire of which Nebuchadnezzar was the guiding light was, in fact, just a flash in the pan. The Assyrians of northern Iraq had ruled for over 400 years, but their successor, Babylon, only lasted 73 years. The ancient kingdom in Iraq did not endure. God had set it up and God took it down. It was as Daniel had declared.

Anyone familiar with the glory years of Saddam Hussein will recall his boastful claims to the legacy of Nebuchadnezzar. Saddam aspired to be the fulfillment of the Neo-Babylonian dream and fashioned himself as the Neo-Nebuchadnezzar. Yet he was up and out in 24 years, and his reputation will live in infamy.

Nebuchadnezzar was every bit the tyrant that his modern counterpart Saddam Hussein had become—only Nebuchadnezzar was more successful than Saddam. The logical connection between the two is inescapable: Two egomaniacal bullies out of the same mold. So then, if it is true as Daniel said—that God gave Nebuchadnezzar his kingdom and God is the one who sets up kings—then the modern emergence of Iraq and the dominant role of Saddam Hussein were most assuredly within the sovereign domain of God's administration.

Though Daniel sprang from the ruling family of Israel, through displacement into Babylon he became the source of undisputed wisdom in ancient Iraq. His prophecies of God's control of history and sovereign disposition over nations are astounding.[5] Daniel knew the score. As chief of the Babylonian Magi, he set the record straight: God is in charge, not Nebuchadnezzar—and in the twenty-first century it was not Saddam Hussein, and not the coalition forces, and certainly not the United States.

God is at work in the affairs of nations. This is the wisdom which comes from the wisest mind of Iraq's past.

WAKING UP TO DESTINY

Where then is the world going? And, is there any rhyme or reason to the coming and going of nations? Ancient civilizations are no longer participants in our modern world, and cartographers are constantly redrawing the maps. It seems that the only constant in the realm of nations and governments is that they are replaced by other nations and governments.

Karl Marx (the father of communism) thought he saw a pattern in this global phenomenon, which he referred to as thesis, then antithesis, then synthesis—to be repeated over and over again. Indeed, many like him have espoused a cyclical view of history, where nations and empires cycle through an observable pattern from ascendancy to complacency to demise.

The Bible on the other hand describes a linear view of history. It is all going somewhere. Sure, there are cycles in the flow of nations, but it's more like a screw than a spinning wheel. A screw goes round and round, yet there is a linear dimension that brings it to a point. History is not a merry-go-round. It is a train on wheels.

In fact, history is about to hit the wall.

Remember the car ads on TV that illustrate the automotive testing procedure for passenger safety and vehicle reliability? A dummy rests comfortably in the driver's seat as the car accelerates toward a wall. Upon impact, the dummy lurches forward, the safety bag explodes out of the steering wheel, and all is well. It's just a demonstration.

In the Bible, however, we read that the nations are hurtling through time toward impact with the Day of the Lord judgment. The apostle John describes the war of Armageddon[6] as a devastating and lethal wall toward which the godless nations are lurching forward like dummies. Only there will be no safety bag and all will not be well. At that time, according to the Bible, God will close the books on history and establish His righteous global Kingdom, defying the pattern of cycles, because it will last forever!

1. Nations in Hibernation

Our existential culture tends to neglect history in favor of concentrating on the present. Perhaps that's why so many people are surprised to learn that Iraq hasn't existed forever. In fact, the entire modern configuration of the Middle East is post-World War I. Prior to then, countries like Syria, Lebanon, Jordan, Saudi Arabia, and Iraq were simply part of the Turkish domain of the Ottoman Empire (1534-1915). Mesopotamia was merely one of the eastern districts.

Ancient Nations Crumble

When war broke out in Europe, the Ottomans aligned themselves with the wrong superpower. Kaiser Wilhelm failed to lead Germany into the Kingdom Age, and the Ottoman Empire crumbled like a dry cookie. For the first time since the Roman Empire, Europe controlled the Middle East. And that's when things began to change.

Moving like a marauding lion, the United Kingdom embraced most of the territory. British troops garrisoned Egypt, Palestine, Transjordan, and what is now Iraq, while the French occupied Lebanon and Syria. Destinies were no longer in the hands of tribal chiefs and Arab warlords. The West would determine what the East was to become.

Following the Great War (as World War I was called), five nations (Britain, France, Italy, Japan, and the United States) drew up a constitution for a League of Nations, to be headquartered in Geneva, Switzerland. A portion of the League's purpose was to oversee the post-war development of the Middle East.

President Woodrow Wilson of the U.S. was the chief architect but, curiously, the United States never joined the League. This multi-national body attempted to monitor the occupations by Britain and France and committed unto them a mandate for future development of the area. So in January of 1920 all was in place to redraw the ancient map of independent countries on the land that stretched from the Mediterranean Sea to the Persian Gulf.

Well, that's how it all happened. After 2500 years of dormancy the great powers of yesterday could be seen rising out of hibernation.

Redrawing the Ancient Maps

Saudi Arabia

Actually, Saudi Arabia's independence predated the War. In 1902 Abd al-Aziz ibn Saud recaptured Riyadh from the Ottomans and over the next few years, regained control of the entire Arabian Peninsula. Then in 1932 Ibn Saud declared that the lands under his control would be known as the Kingdom of Saudi Arabia. A year later he began the development of Saudi Arabia's oil industry.

Iran

On the other side of Iraq, the country of Iran was emerging as the modern version of ancient Persia. During the later years of the 19th Century, Russia and Britain "dominated Iran's trade and manipulated its internal politics."[7] These two European powers never established a colonial rule over Persia, however, but instead used their respective areas for their own interests. In the aftermath of World War I, "Iran was plunged into a state of political, social and economic chaos."[8]

Consequently, in 1919 Britain affirmed Persia's independence and by 1921 Russia backed off as well. Reza Khan then established a military dictatorship and a few years later he was elevated to hereditary Shah of the country. Conditions began to improve and in 1935 "he officially requested all foreign governments to no longer refer to Iran as Persia, but as Iran."[9] So Iran also gained its modern identity in the early years of the 20th Century.

Egypt

On the other end of the Fertile Crescent, Egypt was coming into its own as well. Again British dominion after the War determined the course of Egypt. In 1922 the United Kingdom gave Egypt nominal independence, but it wasn't until 1936 that a renewed treaty with Britain reaffirmed Egypt's autonomy as a nation. Now, Egypt was back.

Syria and Jordan

Syria and Jordan were a little more complicated. After World War I the League of Nations divided greater Syria into Syria (under the French) and Palestine (under the British). Syria was later divided into Lebanon and Syria, while Palestine was separated from Transjordan along the Jordan River.

Yet not until after the Second World War in 1946 did France finally withdraw its troops from Syria and grant the Syrians independent rule. In the same year, England conferred actual independence on Transjordan, having controlled their defenses, foreign affairs, and finances since declaring Transjordan an independent state in 1923. (Transjordan comprises the biblical lands of Ammon, Moab, and Edom—the perpetual enemies of Israel.) In 1949, however, King Abdullah renamed Transjordan "Jordan." Thus, two more ancient kingdoms (Syria and Jordan) were reestablished as modern participants in the Middle East.

Bible Lands Brought Back to Modern-day Prominence

Here's the important thing to note in all of this. Biblically speaking, the thirty year time-frame between the end of World War I and the aftermath of World War II *has been the most strategic period of prophetic fulfillment with regard to the course of nations since the end of the Roman Empire.* The ancient nations that had surrounded Israel in the sixth century BC did not exist again as nations until this involvement by two European powers.

Imposing their influence, the League of Nations (and its post-World War II replacement, the U.N.) carved up the lands of the Bible and brought them back. Gilles Munier states, "These frontiers are the result of a largely artificial plan implemented by the British and the French after World War I."[10]

The sleeping giants had been awakened.

2. Timing is Everything

Times of the Gentiles

In the biblical record, when God closed the pages on Israel's monarchy in the days of Nebuchadnezzar, He invoked a stretch of time in which Gentile nations would rule over the Middle East. Beginning with Babylon's rise to power and sovereign authority over Jerusalem in 605 BC, God anticipated the next 2500 years of Israel's history as a time when other nations would tell them what to do. Luke the historian tells us that Jesus called it "the times of the Gentiles."[11]

The first thousand years of this period are outlined in detail by Daniel in his prophecies. Interpreting the king's dream (Daniel 2) and then his own dream (Daniel 7), Daniel described the succession of empires that would dominate the area. The first two, Babylon and Persia, were local powers. Then, in the hindsight of history, we realized that the next two happened to be European powers.

Daniel used a leopard on the hunt moving quickly to represent Alexander the Great as Alexander imposed the Greek way of life on the entire region. Rome would follow like a devouring monster. Then all appears to decompose for an unspecified length of time as Daniel jumps to the end of the spectrum—a time when God will establish His Kingdom among the nations.

At the point of Rome's dissolution, therefore, it all became a time-warp, like "hold that thought." It's as though God said, "Sometime in the future I'm going to pick up where I left off and bring it all back again." For the next 1500 years we've been waiting.

490 Special Years

Another interesting part of this scenario is the "seventy weeks"[12] prophecy recorded in Daniel's ninth chapter. Following the historical indicators as to when Daniel says this period begins and ends, we realize that the weeks are weeks of years. In other words, there are 70 heptads—or 70 periods of 7 years each—comprising a 490-year stretch of history. This is different than the Times of the Gentiles and refers specifically to Israel's fortune and future within the period of Gentile domination.

Beginning approximately 160 years after the start of the Times of the Gentiles, the "seventy weeks" prophecy began with the return of the Jews to their homeland and the opportunity to rebuild Jerusalem under Persian rule. God was explaining to Israel in the "seventy weeks" prediction that this was the amount of time that He would allow them to live in their land while other nations controlled their destiny.

According to this prophecy of Daniel, an initial 483 years would transpire until the Messiah would come, after which He would be "cut off."[13] And that is exactly what happened. Exactly 483 "prophetic years"[14] after the Jews returned to Jerusalem from Babylonian captivity, Jesus presented Himself as Israel's Messiah and was "cut off" by Roman crucifixion. Daniel's prediction of the succession of nations and his fore view of Israel's future were both being fulfilled as he had said.

There remain seven years unfulfilled, however. Bible teachers refer to this period as "The 70th week of Daniel." According to Daniel, this is the last culminating scenario of world history as we know it. [15] The Jews will be back in their land, historical ethnic and political conditions that were true in the time of Jesus will be restored, and the final showdown between God and the nations will commence.

So, have you followed all of this—the Times of the Gentiles—and the seventy weeks of Daniel? Well, perhaps the following chart will help.

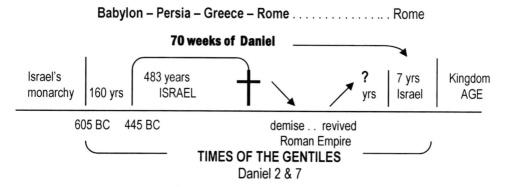

Today's Events in Relationship to Daniel's Seventy Weeks

Now, here is where all of this gets interesting as it relates to the contemporary situation between Iraq and Israel. Before the last seven years of Daniel's "seventy weeks" prophecy can begin, the Bible indicates that the Jews must be back in their land and facing a security problem that only the outside nations can resolve. This seems apparent from Daniel's comment that Israel will depend upon a "covenant" [16] (or security guarantee) by a Gentile ruler.

Ever since the U.N. resolution to grant Israel her national autonomy (1948), Israel has struggled with her Arab neighbors and particularly with the Palestinian problem. After the death of Yasser Arafat, a solution appeared hopeful. However, the rise of radical Hamas as the ruling authority in Gaza has cast a shadow of suspicion over any roadmap to peace. Obviously any solution is going to require a guarantee of Israel's security along the borders of a newly created Palestinian state. The Bible seems to indicate that a world leader will arise who will have the power and authority to make that happen. It seems to many that we are fast approaching that eventuality.

The Middle East

So consider where we are at the opening of the 21st Century. As God predicted, Israel is back as a major player among the nations of the Middle East. Not that Israel is God-fearing and honoring her ancient covenant with God through Abraham—but she is significantly positioned for the beginning of Daniel's 70th week fulfillment.

But not only is Israel back—so are the other ancient nations. It is déjà vu.

Egypt is back as a formidable counterpoint to Israel and so is Syria to the north. Ammon, Moab, and Edom are now represented by the Hashemite Kingdom of Jordan—and, most intriguingly, Babylon has resurfaced as the modern country of Iraq.

Europe

Europe is also back as a unified system and making significant progress as an emerging giant on the world scene. It is not exactly a mirror image of the Old Roman Empire, but the Union did begin in Rome and its political and economic vastness may well exceed the hopes and aspirations of the Caesars.

And don't forget that Europe has a vested interest in the nations of the Middle East. Britain and France determined the boundaries of nations under their respective mandates from the League of Nations and all of Europe has demonstrated an active interest in any future development of the region. To many observers it does seem that the European Union is the rebuilding of a Neo-Roman Empire in progress.

Wide-Eyed Wonder

So, as we look at current conditions in the Middle East, we have to stare in wide-eyed wonder. In a thirty year period of time (1920-1950), the ancient map of Bible times sprang to reality. It was like a blink of an eye—and, *ala kazaam*—there it was! Then, when the newly formed Arab nations invaded Israel on the day it declared its national independence (May 14, 1948), the scenario of end-time events was underway.

The significance in all of this is that the twentieth century appears to have ushered in the beginning of the end of the Times of the Gentiles. How long it will take for God to bring it along to the start of "Daniel's 70th week" conclusion is not known. But it does appear that we have started down the road.

Like Israel, Iraq is back—and that is very significant. The time has come for the end to begin.

Dan Hayden

Chapter Two

SURPRISE! SURPRISE!

The Downfall of Saddam's Regime

People with great power and privilege often forget that the only real authority in the universe resides with the omnipotent all-wise God. This is especially true for kings and queens and presidents and czars. Power can be intoxicating and those who yield to its stupefying influence end up drunk in their own conceit.

That can happen to all of us, of course, but the opportunity to indulge doesn't always knock in our direction. With those to whom it does, the consequences of misconceiving the privilege of authority can be devastating. Caught up in the mirage of self-importance, they are blinded by the delusion that they are in control. They never really are, however—only apparently so.

God is the only sovereign in the universe and His purposes are never thwarted or frustrated. He may allow men and women to persist in their delusions of power for a time, but the moment He chooses otherwise, it's over. They're done . . . or redirected . . . or neutralized . . . or eliminated.

Make no mistake about it. God is in control—always!

Whenever I am frustrated with someone in leadership, my mind gravitates to that wonderful Proverb of King Solomon: *The king's heart is a stream of water in the hand of the LORD; he turns it wherever he will* (Proverbs 21:1).

For a time our family lived on the Wisconsin River in northern Wisconsin. What was so intriguing about the northern part of the river as it flowed south toward central Wisconsin were the cutbacks. It seemed that the water never ran straight. One sharp curve led to another, which led to yet another. And wherever the river banks went, the water dutifully followed. The turns determined the course of the river, not the water.

The proverb says that the king's heart is like the water—subject to external control. God is the one who turns the heart of the king and He can do it whenever and however He chooses. With God, cutbacks are no problem, even 180° reversals. It is good to remember that kings and presidents rule solely at the pleasure of the Almighty. What He allows and what He causes determine the course of their rule.

That is how the Bible would describe what is happening in the Middle East today. Rogues in high places are not forging the future. God is. And that is why Saddam Hussein only ruled for twenty-four years. God allowed him to come to power and then through the instrumentality of the coalition forces, God eliminated him. Saddam Hussein was bound by the limits of God's authority.

SADDAM HAD "NO IDEA"

The genius of the American dream is that a person can come from nowhere and end up somewhere. From poverty to riches, from obscurity to fame—we all love the Cinderella stories of American history.

Remember Abraham Lincoln's log cabin and humble beginnings. Through hard work and perseverance and a large dose of common sense, he rose to the highest office in the land. And as President of the United States, he did not forget his roots. Encouraging the unfortunate and uplifting the downtrodden was woven into the fiber of his being. Americans think of him with fondness and his story still inspires those who hope for more than mediocrity.

As strange as it may sound, Saddam Hussein was the Abraham Lincoln of Iraq. There are so many ways in which he was not like ol' Abe, but in at least one respect the parallel is unmistakable. Like Mr. Lincoln, Saddam emerged out of rural poverty to become the supreme commander of his nation. Saddam *did* forget his roots though, and his brutalities against the people are enshrined in popular regret. In the true mold of other egomaniacal rulers, Saddam aspired to greatness with an obsession. What he ultimately achieved, however, was solitary confinement, incarceration for his sins against humanity, and death by hanging.

In his lust for power, Saddam had protected his interests and manipulated his circumstances, acting as the chief architect of his own destiny. Clawing his way to the top, he gloated over his accomplishments. Iraq had become his personal possession and he was the proud vulture perched over the still-breathing carcass.

Yet Saddam was totally unaware of the fact that God was orchestrating both his rise and his eventual fall. As God said of Pharaoh in the days of Moses, "For this very purpose I have raised you up," [1] so God was accomplishing a divine purpose with Saddam's reign beyond anything Saddam could have imagined.

Saddam presented himself to the world as a supreme ruler with international status. He basked in the light of his ancient historical mentor, Nebuchadnezzar. It was his avowed purpose to duplicate and then surpass Nebuchadnezzar's greatness. Casting himself in the likeness of the ancient king, Saddam aspired to be all that Nebuchadnezzar was—and more. In the end, however, Saddam was more like Nebuchadnezzar than he realized.

Daniel the prophet tells of God's intervention in the affairs of Nebuchadnezzar's kingdom when the Babylonian king was at the height of his success.[2] The king was strutting around his palace boasting of his accomplishments when God struck him with mental illness. For seven years, Daniel says, Nebuchadnezzar wandered in the fields of his kingdom as an animal. His hair and nails grew long. He lapped water from the river, and nibbled on grass. God afflicted him with an insanity that reflected the beastly nature of his heart. Upon recovering from his seven-year ordeal, Daniel says, Nebuchadnezzar finally recognized the sovereign control of God over the affairs of his life and kingdom.

Well, it appears that Saddam Hussein didn't get the point, but he did end up living like an animal in the likeness of his ancient hero. As the coalition forces thundered into Baghdad, Saddam Hussein fled for his life. For nine months he ran and ran, hiding here and there. Then, like a gopher, he found a hole in the ground on a farm in Ad Dawr, a short distance south of Tikrit.

When the Special Forces sniffed him out on the evening of December 13, 2003, he was "resigned, cowering, meek and weak."[3] Six feet beneath the ground in a 6 x 8 hole, the once proud monarch had curled up with his pistol, two AK-47s and $750,000 in one hundred-dollar bills. What emerged from the hole was a "dirty, disheveled man with a matted beard"[4] looking incredibly like the Hollywood image of a werewolf. Saddam had finally achieved his goal of becoming the mirror image of Nebuchadnezzar (but at Nebuchadnezzar's worst moment, not his greatest).

Is God able to exalt and depose human rulers? Of course He is. And according to the biblical perspective that's exactly what happened in Iraq. Saddam Hussein had no idea that God was controlling his destiny.

THE IMPOSSIBLE DREAM

Iraq under Saddam was promised military ascendancy and greatness in the Arab world. It was a personal dream fanned into a fanatical national obsession by the Mad Hatter of Baghdad. Saddam's version of the Neo-Babylonian Empire of the sixth century BC was supposed to rise out of the black mud of Mesopotamia and Iraqis were supposed to enter a utopian age.

At least, that was the plan. The fact that this did not happen was not for lack of effort on Saddam's part. It's just that it was never scripted that way by God.

Saddam's first agenda upon being appointed president of Iraq was to invade Iran. Persia was the ancient enemy of Neo-Babylonianism and Saddam immediately saw an opportunity to capitalize on Iran's political and economic weakness. Humiliating Iran (or Persia) and expanding his eastern boarders would have suited him well. But God allowed the Ayatollah Khomeini to return from exile and establish a formidable Iranian opposition to Saddam's threats.

After two years of war Saddam sued for peace and Khomeini refused. Over the next eight years the war effort squandered Iraq's economy (as well as Iran's) and Saddam found himself heavily in debt to the rest of the Arab world. So far, things were not going well.

The Iran-Iraq war was over in 1989 and one year later Saddam invaded Kuwait. He had always considered Kuwait as the southern part of his kingdom and accused the British of drawing arbitrary lines in the sand when they created Kuwait as an independent nation. Therefore any excuse to annex Kuwait was sufficient for Saddam. He was desperate for Kuwaiti assets, including oil, to pay his war debt.

Misreading diplomatic cues, he assumed the United States would not intervene as his tanks rumbled across the border. But Saddam was wrong again. The U.S. did intervene with an international coalition and Saddam was forced to abandon his expansionist dream. Things were still not going well.

Because the U.S. needed a bad guy in the region to justify a continuing military presence in the Persian Gulf, Saddam was allowed to remain in power. Spinning this as an Iraqi victory, Saddam saw his ejection from Kuwait as a mere setback to his plans for greatness.

Over the next thirteen years he played hide-and-seek with U.N. weapons inspectors and struck deals under the table with France, Germany, and Russia for weapons and technology. Funding for these acquisitions proved not to be a problem. An elaborate scam in the U.N. Oil for Food program bankrolled his efforts. Weapons of mass destruction and nuclear capability were most certainly on his agenda and becoming a powerhouse in the Middle East was still his dream.

Who knows whether he might have succeeded in his grandiose scheme had it not been for the terrorist attack in New York City on September 11, 2001. Osama bin Laden had angered the giant and soon Saddam Hussein was in trouble. As a supporter of terrorism Saddam was again targeted by the West—this time for annihilation. He would be deposed and hunted while his regime would be dismantled. Saddam's dream of greatness had become the ultimate nightmare.

It was the impossible dream. Not because Saddam was a miscalculating klutz aspiring to things beyond his incompetent reach, but because God had an alternate plan for Iraq and Saddam was merely part of His means of getting there.

SETTING THE STAGE

Is it possible that God can accomplish His purposes through the actions of bad people and through unfortunate, even tragic events? Well, the Bible says that He can—and does—without involving Himself in complicity with evil.

Since the first occasion when man introduced sin into the world while attempting to forge his own future independent of divine control,[5] God has been working His sovereign will in the world in spite of mankind's rebellious opposition. Men and women may shake their fists at the sky in defiance of God, but the Bible says that God merely laughs the laugh of scorn and proceeds to confound their ways.[6]

Remember that Saddam Hussein was not the only evil in Iraq. Iraq's short history is plagued by coups, assassinations, a revolution, political graft, personal ambition, and terrorism. It is a difficult place, and like the Wild, Wild West, not easy to tame. But God has been forging a new deal in the ancient land of black mud. Future end-time Babylon is emerging out of the ruins of the past.

So, what has God done in Iraq over the last eighty-five years? Well, just think for a moment about what's been happening.

1. Iraq is a sovereign nation governed by its own people. For almost a century now (longer than the Neo-Babylonian Empire existed), Iraq has been in the process of establishing its modern identity. Obviously God has used the turbulent developmental years of the emergence of this nation to form the psychological and sociological framework of end-time Babylon. It is all becoming what God has determined that it should be.

2. Iraq is no longer a military threat. Saddam's militaristic policies convinced the Arab world and the west that Iraq should not have a military presence among the nations. Interestingly, end-time Babylon is not listed with the other revived ancient countries in the final biblical wars. Babylon is there economically and religiously, but not militarily. Since 2003, we know why.

3. During the Iraq-Iran War, Saddam Hussein began the rebuilding of actual Babylon. His attempt to refashion the Neo-Babylonian Empire of Nebuchadnezzar led him to rebuild ancient Babylon as a symbol for Iraq's emerging greatness. The bombings of two wars have not destroyed what he built and coalition forces are currently using the facilities as a military base of operations. Eventually, though, all is in place to revitalize the project as the ancient symbol of world unity.

4. Religious terrorism has created a climate for desperate measures to find an avenue to religious compromise, not only between the Sunnis and Shiites, but also with other religions of the world. Babylon is the original source of New Age post-modern spirituality and New Agers are infatuated with its symbolic importance. As we move into the days ahead, terrorism may provide the motivation for a cooperative compromise and Babylon could very well become the solution for religious peace in the world.

5. The sympathies of the world are now firmly fixed on Iraq. Sure, the liberal element of the U.S. wants us to get out of there, but everyone is interested in a better life for Iraqis and everyone wants a piece of Iraq's future. Oil is the secular bait, but the strategic location between east and west may be the ultimate key. As a showpiece for democracy (or at least representative government), Iraq could loom large for the future of the Middle East.

6. Europe now has a vested interest in the future of Iraq. Biblical prophecy seems to indicate that Europe will be the superpower of the west in the end-time scenario (a subject I will discuss in later chapters) and will establish a strong connection with commercial and religious Babylon. The United States will apparently become a subservient participant in Europe's greatness and another liberal regime in Washington could make that happen in a hurry. Britain was the principal figure in establishing modern Iraq and continues to seek an active involvement in its future. France and Germany were even willing to undermine American interests in the region for their own economic advantage. Other European nations are involved in the current affairs of Iraq as well. It does seem that conditions are becoming favorable for a major European influence on the future of Iraq.

7. The people of Iraq are ready for a measure of peace and prosperity. The biblical end-time Babylon is a thriving commercial success basking in the popularity of world opinion. All it would take for that to become a reality is religious peace and political cooperation amongst the Iraqi people.

Like Europe over the last sixty years, Iraq would not have to worry about national expenditures for a military budget and could concentrate on economic development. Corralling and increasing her oil production, reestablishing irrigation systems along the Tigris and Euphrates rivers, establishing a commercial port on the Persian Gulf, and catering to historical and biblical tourism would most assuredly put Iraq on the map of prosperity. After decades of economic oppression by tyranny, war and violence, Iraqis are ready for such a scenario. So apparently is the rest of the world.

The Bible has much to say about Iraq's past, present, and future. And all of the above suggestions are consistent with the anticipation of biblical prophecy. Whether reading Isaiah 13 and 14, Jeremiah 50 and 51, or Revelation 17 and 18, we are assured that ancient Babylon will have a significant presence at the conclusion of the Times of the Gentiles. What we have seen and are seeing in Iraq certainly seems to be setting the stage for that fulfillment.

WHERE TO GO FROM HERE

Hopefully this chapter has reminded us that God is in control of the nations and that He is moving them to a point of no return. At the Day of the Lord judgment which culminates in the war of Armageddon, God will destroy the godless nations of the world and establish His Kingdom on the earth. That is the message of the Bible. At that time, end-time Babylon will be destroyed by God with fire out of heaven. The emergence of Iraq out of the mud is part of that story.

Next, however, we need to appreciate the significance of Iraq in the biblical record and familiarize ourselves with what the text actually says about that part of the world. Some people are surprised to learn that the Bible begins in Iraq and ends in Iraq. In fact, Iraq is the starting and finish line of human history. So, turn the page and join me on an incredible journey that will take us back thousands of years to our human roots.

Chapter Three

BABYLON: THE ECLIPSE OF EDEN
It All Began in Iraq

As we approach the end of the age, it is no accident that all eyes are on the Gulf. History demands it and biblical prophecy foretold it.

The record of man's sojourn upon the earth began in a fertile, alluvial plain of this land and according to the Bible the final judgment of God on the kingdoms of mankind in the Day of the Lord will fall unrelentingly upon this historically significant spot of the earth.

To understand the significance of Iraq in the prophecies of the Bible, however, we must go back to ancient times and names forged by civilizations long forgotten. Historians speak of places like Sumer, Akkad, Babylon, and Assyria with important cities such as Ur, Nineveh, and Babylon. In all of this they are describing the territory we now know as Iraq. Biblical prophecies couched in these ancient terms therefore may be referring to events now unfolding in the Gulf under such new names as Iraq and Kuwait.

The fact that Saddam Hussein undertook a three-phase project to rebuild Babylon, located just a short distance southwest of Baghdad, is of great interest to students of the Bible. The wars in the Gulf may also be prophetically significant, especially as they relate to post-war developments in the Gulf region. What does it all mean? Where will it all end? The answer to these common queries will be found in a comprehensive study of the spiritual significance of biblical Babylon.

FROM A GARDEN TO A DESERT

His slender head swayed in rhythmic beauty, casting shimmering rays of iridescent brilliance while his cold black eyes cast a hypnotic spell on the newly created woman. It had been a daring move on his part, slithering into the garden of God so inconspicuously in his serpentine guise. Now his grandest hopes were unfolding as his forked tongue formed the seductive words that would strip the woman of her innocence.

"Hiss-s-s . . . You s-s-surely s-s-shall not die . . . you s-s-s-hall be as God, knowing good . . . s-s-s . . . and evil. S-s-s-s . . ." (Genesis 3:4-5 – KJV).

It was so easy. She was so naïve . . . so willing to comply . . . so eager to be like "Elohim." And what about the man? Well, he might have parried the twisted words of the serpent, but he was no match for the doleful eyes of the woman. Yes, he fell, too. And you know, it all happened in Babylon.

Where in the world was the Garden of Eden located? Numerous theories abound, but according to *The Illustrated Bible Dictionary* the most common opinion is the view that "the garden lay somewhere in S[outhern] Mesopotamia."[1]

Geographical notations in the Bible link the Garden with an extended plain called "Eden" (Gen. 2:8), a Sumerian word indicating that the Garden was situated in "a plain or flat region."[2]

Furthermore, four rivers are associated with this plain in the Genesis account (Gen. 2:11-14): two are unknown (the Pishon and the Gihon), and two are identified "without dissent"[3] with the Tigris and the Euphrates. This is the reason it is commonly thought that the linking of these rivers in the delta region of southern Iraq and Kuwait is the most logical location for this "garden of God" (Ezek. 28:13).

Another line of reasoning that identifies southern Iraq as the location of the Garden of Eden has to do with the tremendous deposits of oil in that part of the world. These oil reserves suggest a former period of lush vegetation in the region.

For instance, an interesting exhibit by the Exxon Corporation at Disney's EPCOT Center demonstrates how primeval rain forests created underground reservoirs of energy resources such as coal and oil, through the decay and sedimentation process accompanied by pressure and time. This would argue for the possibility that the areas above the oil deposits in Iraq, Kuwait, and Saudi Arabia were once a garden spot of the world.

Extreme changes in terrain and climate, from forest to desert and from tropical to arid, could be explained by the tremendous upheavals of land and the hydrological sifting of sedimentary materials that resulted from the biblical flood. In other words, the vegetation on top of the ground was buried deep in the earth by the flood (as sod is turned over by a gardener's spade).

This could also account for the loss of the two rivers as the "fountains of the great deep burst forth" (Gen. 7:11) at the time of the flood. All of this could have come about in a relatively short period of time. There is no question though, that the abundant presence of subterranean oil in that area of the world is supportive of the idea that it was once a place conducive to "a garden in Eden, in the east" (Gen. 2:8).

The real significance of this, however, is more than geographical; it is also spiritual. The sin that has plagued our entire planet over the centuries was injected into the human race in the Garden of Eden located in this region. Somewhere in southern Iraq mankind took its first steps of rebellion against God. In the verdant flats of lower Mesopotamia, the Bible says that Satan initiated his campaign of world domination.

The once beautiful garden of God has become a desolate wasteland of limitless sand—even as the human heart, once a fragrant flower of communion with God, plunged into a lifeless state of spiritual barrenness in Babylonia. This area of the world is the polluted spring from which the contaminated systems of religious perversion have flowed into every crevice of our globe. Is it any wonder that the Bible portrays Babylon as the spiritual symbol of all that is contrary to God and of all that is characteristic of Satan's domain?

THE SAME OLD CESSPOOL

As we continue reading through the biblical record, one event after another ratifies the symbolic nature of Babylon with regard to evil. Adam and Eve were driven from the special garden God had created in the land of Eden, but they probably continued to live in the Eden area.

Ancient historians tell us that Sumer (which is southern Babylonia) was "the earliest and most influential civilization of the ancient Near East."[4] This is certainly consistent with the idea that Adam and Eve set up housekeeping in the general vicinity of the garden from which they were expelled.

Murder and False Religion

In Genesis 4 we read of a tragic incident in which one of their children, Cain, deliberately murdered his brother Abel, due to jealousy and revenge. It is not unreasonable to assume, then, that both murder and false religion (Cain's unacceptable approach to God) had their beginnings in Babylonia. The horrific thoughts and actions that would perpetually plague the human race were formulated in the shadow of Eden.

The Bible goes on to say that Cain left the Eden area and "settled in the land of Nod, east of Eden" (Gen. 4:16). Whether he went to the Far East or merely to the Near East is not said. The implication, however, seems to be that he remained rather close at hand in the territory eventually known as Persia (now Iran).

A civilization of godless people emerged from that transmigration of Cain and his sister-wife. Not until Adam and Eve had another son, Seth, did men begin to "call upon the name of the LORD" (Gen. 4:26). Immediately, however, the corrupting influence of Babylonia permeated the expanding communities of the early world. Antediluvian mankind was evidently rather widespread in the earth, but there are reasons to believe that the next incident in Genesis also had its moorings in the original setting of Babylonia.

The Flood

The conditions that precipitated the worldwide flood seem also to have centered in that part of the world. According to Genesis 5, Noah was of the line of Seth, who appears to have remained in the vicinity of Eden. It's at least possible, then, that Noah built his ark on the plains of Mesopotamia after which, over the period of a year, it floated north to the mountains of Ararat.

Then in Genesis 10, the offspring of Ham (Noah's second son) made a beeline back home to Babylonia where the descendants of Ham (Cush and

Nimrod) revived the heretical religious perversions of their satanically influenced ancestors. Babylonia is the fountainhead of evil, and I am suggesting that it is at least conceivable that the culmination of evil in the pre-flood world had its center in the same old cesspool.

CENTER FOR A UNITED WORLD

Cush, the son of Ham, "is generally represented as having been a ringleader in the great apostasy"[5] that eventually led to the construction of the Tower of Babel (Gen. 11:3-4). His son Nimrod was the first to establish a Babylonian kingdom through his conquests of neighboring areas, and it was Nimrod's wife Semiramis who formulated the anti-God religious system that became the model of religious perversion for the rest of the world.[6]

Thus, there was a segment of Noah's posterity that migrated back to Babylonia and fell prey to the same satanic influence that plagued the pre-flood civilization.

It is in this context (Gen. 11) that we learn of man's attempt to develop a one-world government under the influence of Nimrod—complete with a one-world religion centered in Babylon. In the very place where sin entered the world through Adam and Eve, the Bible indicates that Satan sought to develop a system of political and religious control over the peoples of the earth. Babylon, it appears, was to be the center of world domination, according to the plans of the evil one.

God saw through their plans, however, and scattered the people by confounding their ability to communicate (Gen. 11:9). New language patterns developed, but according to Alexander Hislop in his book *The Two Babylons*, the religious corruption that began in Babylon was adopted into the idolatrous systems of newly developing and migrating cultures, so that "Babylon was the primal source from which all these systems of idolatry flowed."[7]

Even though God had scattered the people over the face of the earth, Babylon continued to serve as a symbol of spiritual corruption. It is in this sense that John refers to Babylon as "BABYLON THE GREAT, THE **MOTHER** OF HARLOTS AND OF THE ABOMINATIONS OF THE EARTH"

(Rev. 17:5, KJV – emphasis mine). Babylon continued to manifest itself as the fountainhead of evil in the world.

CONTRASTING SYMBOLS AND SYSTEMS

It is at this point in the biblical narrative that a significant contrast is developed. The territory of Babylonia (eventually referred to as simply Babylon after its principal city) is recognized by God in the early chapters of Genesis as the center and symbol of world evil (Gen. 3-11). Now a new center, Jerusalem, will come to the fore in the plan of God as the symbol of salvation and righteousness. The development of a new land, a new nation, and blessings to replace cursings (Gen. 12:1-3) is the primary theme of the rest of scripture.

A set of contrasting symbols and systems is thereby introduced into the revelation of God as a means of instructing people concerning the nature of their jeopardy and the opportunity for their salvation.

One of the major cities of Sumer was Ur, a city that reflected all of the satanically inspired influences of the Babylonian system. In order to show the contrast of godliness with evil, God asked Abram (later renamed Abraham) to leave that city and to move around the Fertile Crescent to the land of Canaan. "Go from your country" (Gen. 12:1) is certainly a statement of separation, demonstrating that the blessings of God were to be contrasted with the evils of Babylon.

Another interesting account in the book of Genesis is the story of Abraham's search for a bride for his son Isaac (Gen. 24). A trusted household servant was commissioned with the task of returning to Babylon for the purpose of finding a bride. Abraham's orders to his servant were specific and clear: "You . . . will go to my country and to my kindred, and take a wife for my son Isaac" (Gen. 24:4).

When the servant inquired concerning the possibility of the woman not wanting to leave her homeland and the potential idea of taking Isaac back to Babylon to live, Abraham was adamant: "See to it that you do not take my son back there" (Gen. 24:6). Coming out—and staying out—of Babylon was the only option as far as Abraham was concerned.

Babylon represented all that was evil, and Abraham's primary concerns were to get Rebekah, the bride-to-be, out of there and to keep

Isaac from going back. The same would also be true in later chapters of Genesis as Jacob went in search of a Babylonian wife among the kin of his father and grandfather.

As Babylon represents the apex of evil in the world, so Israel is illustrative of those who are called out of that evil to serve a holy God. Abraham, Isaac, and Jacob were Babylonians, and so were their wives. The twelve tribes of Israel came from the twelve sons of Jacob who were born of four Babylonian women (Leah, Zilpah, Rachel, and Bilhah). The roots of the Jewish people are in Iraq.

The significance of biblical history, however, is that Israel is no longer Babylonian. As the people chosen by God to come out of Babylon, they are in contrast to, and in conflict with, those who remain in Babylon.

The unprovoked Scud attacks on Israel by Iraq during the Desert Storm War, (underscoring the primary and ultimate goal of Saddam Hussein to eliminate Israel from the face of the earth), are certainly contemporary evidences of this contrastive principle of spiritual conflict.

Babylon in the Bible represents the throne of Satan; Jerusalem signifies the throne of Christ. Eden, in Babylon, is the fountainhead of evil; and Golgotha (the place of Christ's crucifixion) in Israel symbolizes the fountainhead of righteousness. Never are there greater extremes or more severe opposites.

THE TALE OF TWO CITIES

Shortly after Abraham arrived in the new land, having separated himself from Babylon, a battle took place that illustrates the contrastive nature of Babylon and Jerusalem as spiritual symbols. Lot had come with Uncle Abraham out of Ur, but he was still infatuated with Babylon's culture and lifestyle. This became clear when he chose Sodom and Gomorrah as the place where he would raise his family (Gen. 13:10-13).

Though he was a righteous man (2 Pet. 2:7-8), he was still enticed by nice things and sensual experiences. Thus, he was in the wrong place at the wrong time and was captured by a coalition of invading kings (Gen. 14:1-2).

The kings of this coalition were from Shinar, Ellasar, Elam, and Goiim—all locations in Iraq. In fact, "All four of these attacking kings were from the region of southern Mesopotamia."[8] This is the area out of which Abraham and Lot had come when they left Ur, so the fact that all were kings of the city states in the region of Mesopotamia is significant in the biblical account. Early in the Genesis record, therefore, we discover conflict between Abraham, the separated one, and the influence of Babylon from which he had separated.

In the story, Abraham pursued the Babylonian kings, and with just 318 of his own servants, overtook and defeated them. He rescued the captives (including Lot and his family) and restored all that had been taken out of Sodom and Gomorrah. Abraham kept only 10% of the booty for himself, which he then gave as a tithe of his victory to the priest of God with whom he had developed an allegiance: Melchizedek, the king-priest of Salem. Many Bible scholars believe that "Salem" was in actuality Jeru**salem**.

Thus, early in the development of Israel's history—long before David made Jerusalem its capital—a contrast was formulated between Babylon, the symbol of evil, and Jerusalem (Salem), the city of Abraham's devotion.

Babylon and Jerusalem. "One is the city of rebellion and warfare, the other a city of peace . . . One is the city of man, the other is the city of God."[9] It is the tale of two systems represented by two cities. It is the biblical account of spiritual contrasts.

SYMBOLS IN CONFLICT

Israel has had many enemies. Yet, two stand out as ultimate foes because they were the powers that ended Israel's monarchy. Both of these nemesis kingdoms occupied the territory we now call Iraq.

Assyria hailed from northern Iraq, with its capital in Nineveh; and Babylon was situated in southern Iraq. Although separate ruling powers, they were bound together by a common thread: the worship of Marduk. Since the Temple of Marduk was in Babylon, all of the Assyrian kings were crowned there. Assyria and Babylon were two peas in the same pod.

This was strikingly similar to conditions in Israel. After the death of King Solomon, civil war broke out in Israel as competing factions struggled for power. Rehoboam (Solomon's son) retained control of southern Israel and Jerusalem, while Jeroboam, a military commander under Solomon, took the ten northern tribes and seceded from the union.

The two factions became known as Judah, to the south, with its capital in Jerusalem, and Ephraim (or Israel) to the north, with its capital in Samaria. As with Nineveh and Babylon, Jerusalem and Samaria were separate powers but two peas from the same pod.

1. Shadow Symbols

What is so interesting in this comparison is how God arranged for each of the Mesopotamian kingdoms to discipline the two factions of Israel. It was north against north and south against south.

Assyria (in the north) became the destroying force against northern Israel and Samaria in 721 BC. Then little more than a century later Babylon (to the south) terminated the Davidic throne in the southern kingdom of Judah and destroyed Jerusalem. There has never been a king on the throne of Judah since that time.

The fascination with all of this continues when we realize that each of these Iraqi kingdoms—Assyria and Babylon—was only allowed to remain in power for the length of time that it took for God to discipline His people.

In the case of Israel's ten northern tribes, the judgment of God appears to have been more severe. When the Assyrians destroyed Samaria (721 BC), the inhabitants of the ten tribes scattered throughout the kingdom of Assyria, never to be heard from again. Undoubtedly this was because of their blatant apostasy. No king of the northern tribes ever came from the genuine lineage of David, nor were any faithful to the God of Israel. Furthermore, the people were idolatrous and pagan in their cultural practices. So God simply removed them . . . and He used Assyria to do it.

Though Assyria was in northern Iraq (there are still Assyrians there today), they were not truly Babylonian in their heritage. In similar fashion, though the ten tribes of Ephraim were in northern Israel, they were not (spiritually speaking) the people of God. Both Assyria and Ephraim were shadow kingdoms—close relatives, but not the real thing.

When Nineveh (Assyria) conquered Samaria (Ephraim), it was merely a fore view of the real thing to come. Then Assyria was gone, fading into the historic past. They had fulfilled their usefulness in the divine plan, and in 612 BC, God replaced them with Babylon when Babylon conquered Nineveh.

2. Genuine Symbols

Babylon was the historic site of Satan's glory years: the introduction of sin into the Garden of Eden, the corruption of the pre-flood civilization and the Tower of Babel with its political and religious conspiracy against the God of heaven. Thus, Babylon is Satan's place and the biblical symbol of satanic rebellion in the world.

So it is no accident that God allowed Babylon to temporarily denude Judah and Jerusalem of its royal throne. In the biblical account, as Satan claimed a temporary victory over Christ at the cross, so Babylon boasted of what became a short-lived victory over Judah.

When Nebuchadnezzar the Babylonian king conquered Judah and deported the citizens of Jerusalem to Babylon at the beginning of the sixth century BC, it was because God had raised him up for the express purpose of doing that.

God was disciplining His people for their prolonged disobedience and, according to the Bible, Nebuchadnezzar became His means of accomplishing it. Jeremiah the prophet explains that the captivity would last for 70 years as a back payment for not observing the Sabbath-year-rest with regard to the land for 490 years (2 Chron. 36:21).

God had instructed Israel to allow the land to lay fallow every seventh year for the purpose of rejuvenating the soil. God promised to provide a bumper crop in the sixth year to carry the people through the non-productive seventh year. This was a divine command with which Israel refused to comply. They simply would not trust God for the seventh year provision. In 490 years of non-compliance, therefore, they owed God 70 Sabbath-year-rests.

So in the Babylonian captivity, God effectively removed them from the land for the 70 years they owed Him. After that, God had determined to return them to their land.

Since the Babylonians would never have agreed to relinquish their grip on Israel, God raised up the Persians to conquer Babylon. It was the

Persians then who allowed Israel to return to their land under Ezra and Nehemiah. The Empire of Babylon had lasted just 73 years—the exact time it took for God to use them in the discipline of His people.

Then, like Assyria, Babylon was gone.

My point is this: Babylon is the same satanic symbol highlighted in the early chapters of Genesis that God had dealt with in the flood. Like Saddam Hussein in our time, the Neo-Babylonian Empire had evil designs against Israel. Because the Jews were the people of God, both tyrannical regimes wanted to terminate Israel's existence. They were satanically inspired and God allowed Satan to gloat over his phantom victories for a time.

But even as Christ arose from the dead in victory over Satan, sin, and death, to one day reestablish the throne of David in the Kingdom Age, so Israel is rising out of the debris of history in defiance of the nefarious plans of Nebuchadnezzar and Saddam Hussein. The drama of the two symbols, Jerusalem and Babylon, has been reenacted in preparation for the dramatic climax of the Times of the Gentiles. It is all as God said it would be.

PARADISE REGAINED

Why are all eyes on the Gulf? Why was the whole world captivated by the personification of evil emanating out of Baghdad? Why was Saddam's greatest hatred leveled at Israel? The Bible reveals that the reasons lie in the restoration of spiritual symbols in God's plan for the end of the age. Not only is Israel back—so is Babylon.

During the Times of the Gentiles, both Israel and Babylon lapsed into a period of historical dormancy. Now, as we approach the end of the age, both are reviving. It is fitting to history; it is fulfilling of prophecy. Israel will be purified and exalted; Babylon will be judged and destroyed.

The paradise of God in the Garden of Eden was eclipsed by sin in the land of Babylon. The Kingdom of Christ, however, will remove the evils of Babylon, as symbolized by its system and city (Rev. 17-18), and will bind Satan, the perpetrator of all that Babylon symbolizes (Rev. 20). In turn, paradise will be restored on earth (Isa. 11) as Jesus Christ, the Son of God, rules upon the throne of David in Jerusalem (Isa. 9:7). That is how the Bible describes what is happening.

What about Saddam Hussein's designs to create an Iraqi empire and destroy Israel? Why wasn't he able to succeed? Well, that's the next part of our story.

Chapter Four

THE EMPIRE THAT WAS
Saddam's Hopeless Dream

Never had they seen so much gold in one place. It was a magnificent structure, rising ninety feet into the air, and pure gold from head to toe. Nebuchadnezzar said it was symbolic of him and his empire, but the three Jewish men who were about to be thrown into a furnace, and Nebuchadnezzar himself, who was doing the throwing—all knew that was a lie. Daniel and his three friends had been instructed by God to tell the king that only the head was made of gold. The rest of the image in his dream was of silver, bronze, iron, and iron mixed with clay (Dan. 2:32-33). Obviously the king had other ideas.

It was flattering to be told that he was the head of gold. Nebuchadnezzar liked that. He liked being the head, and he liked the fact that it was made out of gold. That meant that no one was more important than he. He was on top, and he was the best. What more could a man want? To be the whole image, that's what!

So he made a monstrous sculpture and put it on public display in the province of Babylon (Dan. 3:1). Only he made it all of gold (Dan. 3:5, 10, 12, 14) because that's the way he wanted it to be. The whole world was required to pay homage to this egomaniacal ruler's image (Dan. 3:4-5); and the three Hebrew youths who refused would quickly learn that, for the king, this was no art show. He was diabolically serious. It was his intent that the kingdom of Babylon would reign supreme over the nations of the world throughout the course of history, and he would make sure that everyone agreed with his idea.

There was one serious flaw in his thinking, however—God had other plans. The Babylonian Empire would cease to be and would soon become a "has been" among nations. And so it did. And so it shall ever be.

FLASH IN THE PAN

The story of the Neo-Babylonian Empire of Nebuchadnezzar is a fascinating saga of short-lived glory. At the height of its power, Babylon possessed magnificence unparalleled in the world. A proud complacency, however, led to its early demise. In one generation Babylon gained control over the Middle East, but it took only one more generation for it to cease to exist. From its glorious beginning at the destruction of Nineveh (612 BC) to its infamous ending during the party of Belshazzar (Nebuchadnezzar's grandson), only 73 short years transpired.

Initially Assyria (northern Iraq) ruled over Babylon (southern Iraq). That was the deal for over 400 years.

Then Nabopolassar, Nebuchadnezzar's father, entertained thoughts of rebellion and appointed himself king of the city. This bold move actually succeeded and soon Nabopolassar was threatening the very existence of the Assyrians. Extending his power to the northwest, Nabopolassar struck a deal with the Medes and Scythians. Together they destroyed Nineveh and conquered Assyria. The Neo-Babylonian Empire had been born.

More gifted than his father, Nebuchadnezzar proceeded to fashion Babylon into one of the most spectacular cities of the Middle East. Right along with the pyramids of Egypt, the Hanging Gardens of Babylon enjoyed the reputation of being named one of the Seven Wonders of the Ancient World. Nebuchadnezzar was, in fact, a genius. Yet the most significant aspect of his rule was the extent to which he expanded his conquests to include the land of Israel.

Meanwhile back in Jerusalem things were not going well. Egyptian forces had moved north along the Mediterranean coast to isolate the nation of Israel. In a decisive battle at Megiddo (609 BC), Pharaoh Necho of Egypt murdered King Josiah of Israel—and suddenly Israel faced a new boss. Egypt was flexing its territorial muscles.

Shortly after that Nebuchadnezzar actually came to power in Babylon (605 BC) and Pharaoh Necho saw an opportunity to take advantage of the young, fledgling king. Conquering Israel had been easy. And in his mind, Babylon would be next. So he marched his army north out of Israel with his destructive sights firmly fixed on Nebuchadnezzar. As it turned out, this was not a good idea.

When Nebuchadnezzar learned of Pharaoh Necho's plans, he immediately accepted the challenge and moved his army west into Syria to engage the Egyptian forces at Carchemish. As ancient battles go, it wasn't much of a fight. The rumble turned into a rout, with the Egyptians fleeing for their lives. A spirit of panic quickly spread to encompass the Egyptian occupying forces in Israel, who also evacuated the area, like roaches scurrying from a lighted room.

The Babylonians swept south in pursuit of the Egyptians with virtually no resistance. In the process, Nebuchadnezzar became the proud possessor of the little, beleaguered country of Israel. This was the beginning of the Times of the Gentiles. Nineteen years later (586 BC), after a great deal of frustration with the disloyal vassal kings he had left to rule in Jerusalem, Nebuchadnezzar destroyed the Jewish capital and laid to ruins its magnificent temple.

The Babylonian Empire was at the peak of its success as the Times of the Gentiles began. Nebuchadnezzar had become the golden head who inaugurated an extended period of time in which Gentile kingdoms would rule, not just in the Middle East, but especially over Israel and the glorious city of God. His Golden Empire would be short-lived, however. Three other empires would eventually come and go before the consummating Kingdom of Christ would be established in the world.

At no time, though, would the kingdom of Babylon be revived. The city would live again, but not the empire. Jesus Christ alone is the conqueror who was, and who is, and who is to come (Rev. 1:8; 4:9). The Babylonian kingdom is merely "the empire that was."

THE EMPIRE STRIKES OUT

But, will the Babylonian Empire ever rise again? Nebuchadnezzar thought the empire would last forever, but it didn't. Saddam Hussein tried to bring it back, but he couldn't. So what does the future hold? Will someone else succeed where they failed? The **city** of Babylon has been revived, and one can find prophetic reasons for believing that it will enjoy a measure of renewed prominence in the days ahead. But will there be a new **empire in the future**? Recent developments in the Persian Gulf cause us to ask this question with more than academic interest.

What is an Empire?

First of all we need to understand what is meant by an "empire." When a ruling monarch is successful in conquering and controlling a substantial number of other countries, he has established an empire. The difference between a country (or kingdom) and an empire is more than mere size. It is the fact that one nation has expanded its governmental control over other nations by bringing them under its sovereign dominion that qualifies it for empire status: e.g., the Roman Empire, the Ottoman Empire, the British Empire.

This is what Nebuchadnezzar did when he established the Babylonian Empire at the end of the seventh century BC. It is what Saddam Hussein attempted to do at the end of the twentieth century AD, but failed to accomplish.

Saddam's Plans

Some have suggested that Saddam Hussein had definite plans to pursue an expansionist policy beyond taking the little country of Kuwait. For almost a decade he had tried to move his borders east into Iran without success. Then he turned his attention south and overran Kuwait. What appeared to be a sudden and impulsive act, however, was evidently the first step in a series of calculated moves to gain control over the entire Middle East.

<u>Jack Wheeler</u>

According to Jack Wheeler, a senior fellow at the Council for Inter-American Security in Washington D.C., "Saddam Hussein's seizure of Kuwait was undoubtedly only part of a much larger scheme to dismember Saudi Arabia."[1] In an article titled "Unraveling Iraq's Real Agenda," Wheeler explained that four conspirators plotted to gain control over Saudi Arabia.

Saddam Hussein was the chief instigator and beneficiary who was to take Kuwait and then "move fast down the east coast of Saudi Arabia to seize the province of Al-Hasa, which has the enormous oil fields of Hofuf and Dhahran."[2] Yasser Arafat of the Palestinian Liberation Organization "was to have his PLO agents at the banks turn over Kuwait's international assets to Iraq's Hussein."[3] These moves alone would have given Saddam Hussein control over half the world's oil and $200 billion of Kuwaiti assets.

Jordan's King Hussein was evidently a co-conspirator who had designs to regain "the lands he feels were stolen from his family by the Saudis."[4] In coordination with Saddam Hussein's movements, the Jordanians were preparing to move down the west coast of Saudi Arabia into the Hejaz area to absorb the Muslim holy cities of Mecca and Medina. Far to the south, Mohsin Alaini of Yemen had agreed to invade "the Saudi provinces of Asir, Najran and Jaizan,"[5] which were once a part of Yemen but had been annexed by the Saudis in 1934. Jack Wheeler summarized the plans by saying:

> Mohsin was ready to pounce on Asir, Najran and Jaizan, as Saddam Hussein seized Al-Hasa, and King Hussein took the Hejaz, leaving the Saudis with little more than the sands of the Empty Quarter in the center.[6]

Elaine Sciolino

Confirmation of Jack Wheeler's analysis of Saddam's plans can be found in Elaine Sciolino's stirring account of the Kuwait invasion, in which she pictured the Iraqi forces ready to pounce on the unsuspecting Saudis. As a diplomatic correspondent for the *New York Times* (Washington Bureau), she reported that at one point CIA Director Webster telephoned President Bush "to insist that an invasion of Saudi Arabia was imminent."[7] A massive Iraqi troop buildup on the Saudi border had convinced both the U.S. led coalition and Saudi Arabia's King Fahd that an Iraqi invasion was no longer "an abstract problem" but an "immediate threat to Saudi sovereignty."[8]

Sciolino described General Colin Powell's analysis of the situation:

He saw that Saddam's action might be likened to Hitler's invasion of Central Europe in the 1930s—an aggressive dictatorship determined to swallow its neighbors while the rest of the world dithered about what to do. Armed with maps, charts, and satellite photographs, he painted a chilling picture of how easily and quickly Iraq had overrun Kuwait. Crucial Saudi pipelines and refineries were less than 100 miles south across the desert from Kuwait, and one major offshore Saudi oil field, Safaniya, was only about 40 miles from the border. Saddam had nothing to stop him if he wanted to continue his march.[9]

It was this realistic concern, in fact, that convinced King Fahd to invite U.S. forces onto Saudi Arabian soil. Saddam Hussein was definitely threatening to invade Saudi Arabia in order to gobble up the Saudi oil assets and the Saudis knew it.

Yasser Arafat's complicity with Saddam's take-over of Kuwait was obvious. According to Sciolino, "Arafat . . . flew to Baghdad the day after the invasion and was seen on television throughout the Arab world embracing Saddam."[10] King Hussein of Jordan's involvement, on the other hand, was more covert, yet highly suspicious. Jordan had developed close ties with Iraq during the Iraq-Iran war and King Hussein stood to benefit greatly by Saddam's successes. Sciolino describes King Hussein's agenda as "murky," then adds,

Washington's longtime friend, the quintessential Arab moderate in the eyes of the West, he became an apologist for Saddam. Even after the invasion, he called the Iraqi leader "a person to be trusted and dealt with...an Arab patriot in the eyes of many."[11]

Bush's most frustrating calls were the ones to his longtime friend King Hussein. Bush tried, without success, to convince the monarch to abandon Saddam, proving the limits of personal diplomacy.[12]

Ending her discussion of the Arab League's concern over the Kuwait issue, Elaine Sciolino concludes, "With the staunch support of Jordan, the two Yemens, Libya, and the PLO, Saddam Hussein had begun to eclipse both Egypt's Mubarak and Saudi Arabia's Fahd as the leader who set the political agenda for the region."[13]

Saddam's Failure

There's no question about it. Saddam was determined to rebuild the empire of Nebuchadnezzar. And both Jack Wheeler and Elaine Sciolino have revealed how he planned to do it.

If this plot had succeeded, Saddam Hussein would have established undisputed control over the Middle East. Jordan and Yemen would have been puppet regimes, Saudi Arabia and Kuwait would have been added to Saddam's holdings, and he would thus have had the combined military power and financial resources to attempt his ultimate goal of destroying Israel. Having returned the land of Israel to the Palestinians, under Yasser Arafat's leadership, he would then have been in a position to intimidate the rest of the Arab world to acquiesce to his leadership. The Babylonian Empire would have been reborn.

The rebuilding of the city of Babylon and Saddam's Hussein's infatuation with Nebuchadnezzar were all part of this grandiose scheme. It appears that the Iraqi ruler had a revived Babylonian Empire in mind from the beginning. A news article titled "Rebuilding Babylon," in Christianity Today magazine, reporting on Charles Dyer's visit to Iraq in 1988, revealed the connection between the city of Babylon, Nebuchadnezzar, and the empire dream of Saddam Hussein:

> Dyer says Babylon and Nebuchadnezzar appear to be important symbols for the Iraqi president, Saddam Hussein...because it unites them against their two current enemies, Iran and Israel. It was the Persians (Iranians) who destroyed the Neo-Babylonian empire of Nebuchadnezzar, while the Jews were once decisively defeated by inhabitants of the present-day Iraq.[14]

In other words, the city of Babylon had become the symbol of a revived Babylonian Empire that would rule over the lands of Persia (Iran) and Israel.

The Desert Storm War (1991) prevented Saddam Hussein from accomplishing this plan. Yet, he was allowed to remain in power in Iraq and saw his defeat as merely a setback. For the next twelve years he scammed and connived, as we now know, with the U.N. Oil for Food money, to rebuild his military potential and revive his empire dream. Then, in the Iraqi Freedom War (2003) all of that came to a screeching halt. Saddam Hussein was dethroned and the Iraqi military was dismantled. All possibilities and hopes for a new Babylonian Empire went up in the smoke of coalition bombs. Saddam had struck out. There was to be no empire.

IN THE HANDS OF THE LORD

What force is at work in the flow of history that continues to keep this empire in check? Were the coalition forces of the Gulf Wars a mere product of random history, or were they a tool of God to accomplish His sovereign purpose?

The prophet Daniel makes it quite clear that history is the outworking of a divine plan. In Daniel, chapters 2 and 7, the course of Gentile world history is delineated with incredible accuracy and detail. Daniel is not telling us that God simply knows historical events before they happen. He is telling us that God exercises sovereign control over national and international affairs.

Anticipating the Flow of Nations

In Daniel 2 we discover four basic metals symbolizing four successive empires. They are associated with a large image that represents the course of world history during the Times of the Gentiles. Speaking to Nebuchadnezzar, Daniel said:

> You, O king, the king of kings, to whom the God of
> heaven has given the kingdom, the power, and the might,
> and the glory, …you are the head of gold. Another kingdom

inferior to you shall arise after you, and yet a third kingdom of bronze, which shall rule over all the earth. And there shall be a fourth kingdom, strong as iron... (vv. 37-40).

Most conservative evangelical Bible teachers agree that the four empires referred to by Daniel are the Babylonian, the Medo-Persian, the Greek, and the Roman Empires—in that order. The same succession of empires is indicated by the four beasts in Daniel 7 where we read that "These four great beasts are four kings who shall arise out of the earth" (Dan. 7:17). With regard to these kingdoms, Robert Culver makes a summary comment:

> Among Christian interpreters, as long as there has been any record of opinion, the almost uniform identification of the four successive kingdoms has been Babylon, Medo-Persia, Greece, and Rome.[15]

No Revival of the Babylonian Empire

In Daniel 2 the king's dream is analyzed, and the resultant analysis is *political* in nature, with the various metals representing the different governmental strengths and natures. In Daniel 7 the prophet Daniel is the recipient of the comparable dream. There the interpretation reflects a *spiritual* analysis by revealing the beastly nature of each governmental system.

In each case there are only four empires and none of the empires is a repeat of a previous one. The point is that when the Babylonian Empire came to an end in 539 BC it had fulfilled its God-ordained destiny as the head of gold (Dan. 2) and the lion with eagle's wings (Dan. 7). It then ceased to exist, having been replaced by other empires.

Both visions (Nebuchadnezzar's and Daniel's) end with reference to a fifth empire, which is the Kingdom of Christ established in the world. This final empire comes suddenly and with great force to eliminate and replace the empires that have preceded it. In each vision the Gentile empire in existence during the termination of this Gentile domination is the fourth empire (the Roman), not the first empire (the Babylonian). Therefore, the Roman Empire will be revived in the end, not the Babylonian Empire.

Thus, there is no room in the prophecies of Daniel for a resurgence of the Babylonian Empire in the Middle East. Saddam Hussein's failure to accomplish his grandiose dream could have been predicted by reference to Daniel's writings. It may also be said that no other Iraqi opportunist will succeed in accomplishing what Saddam Hussein failed to do. God will see to that.

A revived Babylonian Empire just isn't in the plan.

CONSPICUOUS BY ITS ABSENCE

In the final battles at the end of the age Babylon is conspicuous by its absence. Many of the ancient kingdoms of the Mediterranean rim and the Middle East emerge again in the Bible as combatants in the last wars—but not Babylon. This is all the more striking when we realize that the city of Babylon becomes a prominent center of economics and religion for the end-time society (Jer. 50-51; Rev. 17-18). As the curtain falls at Armageddon, Babylon is situated strategically among the nations of the world, yet it plays no part in the military struggles.

What happens to the kingdom of Babylon to eliminate it from the arena of international conflict? Perhaps the answer is to be found in the recent dismantling of the Iraqi war machine by the coalition forces. Perched on the brink of its imperial dream, with designs to make a mockery of the God of Israel, the modern kingdom of Babylon (Iraq) was reduced to almost nothing. In the post-war developments, every attempt was made to thoroughly eliminate Iraq's war potential. Saddam Hussein not only lost the war, he also incurred the deliberate emasculation of his military power by the nations of the world. His dreams of a Babylonian empire have literally gone up in smoke. In all of this, Daniel the prophet continues to say, *I told you!*

The Gulf War appears to have been another of those momentous events in recent years that have contributed to the divine preparation of the stage of history for the final conflicts that will bring an end to the Times of the Gentiles. The war with Iraq was not Armageddon—neither was it the fulfillment of any other end-time battle. It was the definite fulfillment of prophecy, however. By eliminating Iraq as a military threat to Israel, the Gulf War explained a missing ingredient in many prophecies. Babylon is missing in the final wars. Daniel tells us *why*. The Gulf War tells us *how*.

THE SPIRIT OF THE EMPIRE

So, Nebuchadnezzar's Babylonian Empire does not rise out of the dust of Mesopotamia in the same fashion as does the city of Babylon. The empire of Babylon is the empire that was. It ran its brief course according to the plan of God and then ceased to exist. All the king's horses and all the king's men cannot put it back together again. It is gone—forever!

This does not mean, however, that the spirit of the Babylonian Empire is dead. Quite the contrary! It is very much alive. Saddam Hussein's attempt to resurrect the territorial aspect of the empire failed. Daniel's prophecies would have been inaccurate had he succeeded. The spirit of the empire is not territorially limited, though, but is actually resident in every "antichrist" philosophy of human government. It is in this regard that the final stage of Daniel's fourth empire (Roman) will reflect a Babylonian influence.

In the Book of Revelation, the apostle John describes the Antichrist and his godless system of government in the terms of Daniel's vision of the beasts:

> And I saw a beast rising out of the sea, ...And the
> beast that I saw was like a leopard; its feet were like a
> bear's, and its mouth was like a lion's mouth (Rev. 13:1-2).

The "beast . . . out of the sea" in John's vision is the last and greatest monarch of the Times of the Gentiles. He is the climactic ruler of the revived aspect of the fourth empire, which is the Roman Empire. The interesting thing to notice, however, is that John sees him as embodying the characteristics of the other three empires—sort of a culminating amalgamation of all the empires in the finale of Gentile rule.

Using the beasts of Daniel 7 (in reverse order), John says that the revived Roman Empire will conquer like Alexander's Greeks (leopard – v. 6), will be powerful like Cyrus's Persians (feet of a bear – v. 5), and will talk (and thus, think) like Nebuchadnezzar's Babylonians (mouth of a lion – v. 4). In other words, though the man, Antichrist, is the ruler of a revived European confederacy, he will be energized by the spirit of the Babylonian Empire.

This is all very logical, of course, in that the master spirit behind the Babylonian system, according to the Bible, is the same spirit that will energize the Antichrist—Satan! John refers to him as "the dragon" and describes the Antichrist and his imperial system by saying, "And to it the dragon gave his power and his throne and great authority" (Rev. 13:2). No wonder, then, that the Antichrist will think like a Babylonian. The spirit of Babylon is the spirit of Antichrist—and the spirit of Antichrist is the spirit of Satan.

LET'S PAUSE FOR A MOMENT

Having considered Saddam Hussein's empire dream for Iraq and the slamming of the door on that opportunity, we now need to look at what the Bible says about the city of Babylon. Here again the Bible is clear. Even though the empire was squelched in keeping with Daniel's prophecy, the city of Babylon still seems destined for greatness.

Before we go on with these reflections on Iraq's future, however, we need to pause and consider another striking prophecy by one of Israel's lesser-known prophets. Habakkuk lived in the later days of Israel's monarchy (est. 630 - 580 BC) as a contemporary of the great prophet Jeremiah. In his time, Babylon was just beginning to exercise its independence as a territory of the Assyrian Empire and Habakkuk saw this as a dark omen for the kingdom of Judah. Troubled by the revelations he was receiving from God, Habakkuk began to argue with God over what God was intending to do. In the process he unfolded the prophecies that God was giving him with regard to the emerging threat in Babylon.

Some have thought that Habakkuk's prophecies went far beyond the events of the seventh century BC in the conquest of Israel by Nebuchadnezzar. In fact, they suggest that Habakkuk may have been envisioning Saddam Hussein's invasion of Kuwait.

Sound fantastic? Well, maybe we should stop and look for ourselves.

Chapter Five

GHOST OF KUWAIT
The Prophecy of Habakkuk

Hitler had just invaded Czechoslovakia and Poland, and the Second World War was brewing in Europe. It was 1939 and, in America, my father neared the completion of his seminary education in a small, non-accredited school in upstate New York. Going on for further studies and a degree seemed to be the logical next step for him, but the turmoil of world events put a crimp in any plans he had for the future.

As is the case so often when significant events happen in the world, the Christian community became obsessed in those days with the possibilities of fulfilled prophecy. The word was out: Hitler was the Antichrist and Jesus would be coming soon. Events in Europe seemed to indicate that we were approaching the end of the age and Bible teachers spread the word that Christians should be on red alert.

As World War II came to a screeching halt with the suicide of Hitler and the bombing of Nagasaki and Hiroshima, it was embarrassingly obvious that the prophetic prognosticators were wrong. Hitler was not the Antichrist, and neither was Mussolini.

A few years later Israel became a nation and the prophetic preachers went crazy again. But the 50s were a time of burgeoning prosperity in America, in spite of the Korean War, and the Christian community simply settled down to enjoy the "good life."

In the process, though, my dad had become more guarded about jumping on the prophetic bandwagon. Legitimate prophecy was one thing. Sensational interpretations were another.

Over the years of my ministry I have watched the same unfortunate phenomenon repeated over and over. In 1967 Israel finally won control of Jerusalem in the Six Day War and the prophetic frenzy escalated yet again. You know the hype, right?

Then in 1988 Edgar C. Whisenant created a furor with his calculation that Jesus was coming in that year. In 1989 he revised his prediction, admitting that he was off by just one year. Actually, it's going on twenty years now. How embarrassing! Harold Camping wrote a book saying that the year of Jesus' coming was 1994—absolutely! Well, wrong again. You'd think they'd learn.

With much of this Christian baggage haunting my mind, I received an interesting phone call in 1990. Saddam Hussein had just invaded Kuwait and the excited voice on the other end of the line laid out her recent observations. "Pastor Dan, I think what's happening in the Gulf is a fulfillment of Habakkuk's prophecy. You've got to read it. It's amazing!"

Well, I was interested but very skeptical. Actually, I was impressed that the woman had read the book of Habakkuk. Not many people do. As I reread Habakkuk's short prophecy though, it became apparent to me why this lady was so excited.

Many similarities can be found in comparing what happened in the Desert Storm War to the prophecies of Habakkuk. Hussein's crazy antics seemed to jump off the page. Yet, that spirit of caution prevailed. I was not about to jump to conclusions. Nevertheless, my curiosity had been piqued. Could it be true that Habakkuk was speaking of events in the Middle East at the end of the twentieth century?

UNDERSTANDING THE PROPHET

Before we look at specific prophecies and their possible fulfillment, it will be important for us to get a feel for Habakkuk's purpose. To whom was he referring when he talked about "the Chaldeans"? And why was he so concerned about a distant nation in the midst of his own turbulent setting? Answering these two questions will go a long way in orienting us to what he wrote.

1. Chaldea is Southern Iraq

Learning the ancient names for modern places can be somewhat disconcerting, but with a little patience, they too become familiar. One of the old names for southern Iraq is "Chaldea." (Abraham's city of Ur was a Chaldean city, and Nebuchadnezzar the famed conqueror from Babylon was a Chaldean.)

The Akkadians, one of the ancient cultures of southern Mesopotamia, used the word "kaldu" for that region; then when the Greeks translated the Hebrew Old Testament into Greek, they translated the Akkadian word "kaldu" with the Greek transliteration, "chaldaioi." This in turn came down to us in English as "Chaldea."

So, when we read the prophecy of Habakkuk in our English versions, we read, "For behold, I am raising up the Chaldeans . . ." (1:6). Immediately then, we know to whom Habakkuk is referring. Habakkuk is quoting God as saying that He is raising up the people of southern Iraq, the Chaldeans, who later became known as the Babylonians. The Book of Habakkuk is indeed a prophecy concerning southern Iraq.

2. Habakkuk's Problem

Habakkuk begins his little three chapter book by telling us that he has a problem: "The oracle [or, burden] that Habakkuk the prophet saw" (1:1). Burdened because of the great sin of the people of Judah, to whom he was writing, Habakkuk cried out, asking God to discipline them:

> 2 O LORD, how long shall I cry for help,
> and you will not hear?
> Or cry to you, "Violence!"
> and you will not save?
> 3 Why do you make me see iniquity;
> and why do you idly look at wrong?
> Destruction and violence are before me;
> strife and contention arise.
> 4 So the law is paralyzed,
> and justice never goes forth.
> For the wicked surround the righteous;
> So justice goes forth perverted.

Now, that's pretty strong language. Habakkuk is indeed upset. "Things are really bad, God. Please do something about it!" But he is certainly not prepared for what comes next.

God tells Habakkuk that He is also angry with the wickedness of His people and that He intends to chastise them by "raising up the Chaldeans" (v. 6) against them. In other words, the people of southern Iraq (or Babylon) will be the whipping stick that God will use to discipline Judah.

Well, that's hard for Habakkuk to take. He evidently expected God to do something directly out of heaven—to strike them with a plague or something. What he didn't expect was for God to use a nation more sinful than Judah to be the means of His judgment.

So Habakkuk begins to argue with God (vv. 12-17) and in effect says, "God, how can you do that? This doesn't seem right!" Then Habakkuk determines that he will sit down in his tower and wait for God to answer him (2:1).

God does answer Habakkuk (2:2-20) and tells him not to be so proud, for a man who is truly just would know how to trust God to do what is right. Then God reviews all the evil actions of Judah as a demonstration that He is certainly justified in using the Chaldeans to bring His judgment upon them.

The last chapter of Habakkuk is the prophet's response to what God has just said. Habakkuk finally understands that God can do whatever He wants to do—even if it means bringing a heathen nation out of Iraq to discipline His own people in Jerusalem.

AT FIRST GLANCE

When God revealed his plans as to how He was going to answer Habakkuk's request to discipline Judah, it was a jolting experience for the prophet. Assyria had been the ruling power in Mesopotamia, not Chaldea. So the idea that God would raise up the Chaldeans as a threatening force against Judah seemed farfetched. Nothing of what God said to Habakkuk would have seemed plausible were it not for that fact that it was God speaking. The whole prophecy, therefore, was futuristic. Habakkuk was being asked to look into the future in order to see things that were not yet realistic expectations.

Could it be, then, that the prophet was looking farther into the future than we thought? Was God really—or also—describing events at the end of the twentieth century when the Chaldeans would be called Iraqis? Instead of the hostilities of Nebuchadnezzar, perhaps He was describing the madness of Saddam Hussein. Consider these possibilities from Habakkuk 1.

1. Amazing events—who would have thought?

> v. 5 – Look among the nations, and see; wonder and be astounded. For I am doing a work in your days that you would not believe if told.

King Fahd of Arabia expressed this very thought. He said, "Saddam [Hussein] did the unthinkable" [1] (one Arab country invading another Arab country). Therefore Fahd also had to do "the unthinkable" by inviting infidel forces (U.S. troops) onto Saudi Arabian soil in order to protect his people. Who would have believed it?

2. Possessing places not their own

> v. 6 – For behold, I am raising up the Chaldeans, that bitter and hasty nation, who march through the breadth of the earth, to seize dwellings not their own.

Saddam's expansionist policy to gobble up his neighbors—first Iran, then Kuwait, and ultimately Saudi Arabia—is certainly fitting here.

3. He will be a law unto himself

> v. 7 – They are dreaded and fearsome; their justice and dignity go forth from themselves.

Saddam defied Arab trust by snubbing the principle of solidarity within the Arab League. He cared nothing for the sovereign rights of his neighbors and he thumbed his nose at the rest of the world by ignoring U.N. sanctions and resisting U.N. inspections. He was indeed a law unto himself.

4. Well-armed and prepared for war

> v. 8 – Their horses are swifter than leopards, more fierce than the evening wolves; their horsemen press proudly on. Their horsemen come from afar; they fly like an eagle swift to devour.

Horses were the means of ancient warfare and therefore Habakkuk was limited in his ability to describe Saddam's forces. Using modern terminology, the Iraqi army was well equipped and moved their tanks and ground forces extremely fast into Kuwait. After the Iraq-Iran war, Iraq had the largest army in the Arab world.

5. Taking captives and holding hostages

> v. 9 – They all come for violence, all their faces forward. They gather captives like sand.

John Major, the British Prime Minister during the first Gulf War, commented, "It is perfectly clear that this man is amoral. He takes hostages. He attacks population centers. He threatens prisoners. He is a man without pity, and whatever his fate may be, I for one will not weep for him."[2]

6. Defying other nations and mocking their leaders

> v. 10 – At kings they scoff, and at rulers they laugh. They laugh at every fortress, for they pile up earth and take it.

Saddam Hussein had disregard for the Arab alliance and expressed total disdain for the U.S. and the West. When defying U.N. resolutions, he was mocking the nations of the world.

7. They attribute their strength to their god

> v. 11 – Then they sweep by like the wind and go on,
> "guilty men, whose own might is their god!"

Saddam Hussein and the Iraqi army gave credit to Allah for their victories and waged war with other nations in the name of Allah.

As you can see, it can be rather tempting to interpret the prophecies of Habakkuk in the light of modern events in Iraq. In 1990, when the Gulf conflict first emerged, many were fascinated with these prophecies, wondering if Habakkuk was indeed a prophet speaking of our times.

MORE CONNECTIONS WITH HABAKKUK

As I read on in Habakkuk, other prophecies emerged as though highlighted with contemporary significance. Familiarizing myself with the history of Iraq's eight-year-war with Iran and the details of the later Kuwait invasion, I began to see situations and expressions resembling Habakkuk's poetic verse. With the first glance similarities of verses 5-11 still fresh on my mind, I was arrested with a whole new set of possibilities as I came to the end of chapter one and the early verses of chapter two.

The Victory Arches of Saddam

Iraq and Syria are unique in the Middle East as major Arab nations without a deepwater port. Saddam Hussein understood the problem and felt severely hampered by this restriction, especially as it related to oil exports. As historian Phebe Marr put it, Iraq is "like a man with huge lungs but a tiny windpipe."[3] Saddam was suffocating and the culprits choking his progress were Iran and Kuwait.

This was one of the reasons Saddam declared war on Iran. True, he bore hatred for the land of ancient Persia and would have liked nothing better than to expand his territory into Iran. But a more pressing concern was Iran's resistance to Iraq's use of the water inlet of the Euphrates River from the Persian Gulf.

As the Tigris and Euphrates rivers merge in southern Iraq on their way to the Gulf, the last 130 miles are the borderline between Iraq and Iran. The Iranian side is known as the Shatt al-Arab, and Saddam was desperate to control this region for unhindered access to the Persian Gulf. In fact, in 1982 "one of the biggest battles since World War II"[4] took place at Khorramshahr in the northern part of the Shatt al-Arab. This area was key to Saddam's hope for a deepwater port and the development of an Iraqi Navy.

The end of the Iraq-Iran War turned out to be a stalemate. Yet, in typical Saddam fashion, the eight-year-conflict was spun as a great victory for Iraq. To celebrate Iraq's "victory," Saddam designed two huge monuments of his arms (131 feet tall) to be placed at the entrance and exit of a parade ground in the center of Baghdad. These were called Victory Arches, and featured a nautical theme with nets that attached to each of the arms.

> Perhaps what was most interesting about the Victory Arches was the bright-green helmets—5,000 of them in all—that spilled out from nets attached to each arm. They were taken from the bodies of dead Iranian soldiers, and many of them were riddled with shrapnel and bullet holes. …Saddam intended the monuments to be understood as symbols of renewed imperial ambitions, of Iraqi's power and defiance.[5]

As I read this grotesque account of Saddam's Victory Arches with Iranian helmets suspended in a net entwined about Saddam Hussein's arms, I was drawn to Habakkuk's poetic dirge at the end of chapter one:

> **14** You make mankind like the fish of the
> sea, like crawling things that have no ruler.
> **15** He brings all of them up with a hook; he
> drags them out with his net; he gathers them
> in his dragnet; so he rejoices and is glad.

16 Therefore he sacrifices to his net and makes offerings to his dragnet; for by them he lives in luxury, and his food is rich.
17 Is he then to keep on emptying his net and mercilessly killing nations forever?

The similarity between Saddam Hussein's Victory Arches as the symbol of his supposed victory over Iran and Habakkuk's plaintive description of the Chaldeans (using the imagery of fishing nets) was indeed striking. The question loomed in my mind. *Could this be a prophetic picture of Saddam's skewed view of his war with Iran?* The fact that Saddam's was not a real victory, seemed rather odd to me in that Habakkuk appeared to be describing an actual conquest of their foes by the Chaldeans. Yet, in the light of the earlier verses of chapter one, it was certainly an interesting observation.

Saddam's Indebtedness

At the conclusion of the Iran-Iraq War, Saddam Hussein still hadn't obtained unhindered access to the Persian Gulf. Iran still controlled the Shatt al-Arab, which made it difficult for Iraq to use the mouth of the Euphrates for commercial or military purposes.

Possessing Kuwait seemed like another possibility with its hundreds of miles of Gulf Coast. In addition to his need for access to the Gulf, Saddam had another gargantuan problem. He had spent so much money on the war with Iran that his economy teetered on the verge of bankruptcy and he was seriously in debt. He needed money—and lots of it.

According to the Committee Against Repression and for Democratic Rights in Iraq (CARDRI),

Iraq's total external debt in 1980 was only $2.5 billion. By 1984 it had reached $55 billion. It then climbed to $65 billion in 1985, $75 billion in 1986 and $80 billion by the end of 1987. A very large but undisclosed proportion of Iraq's debts are to Saudi Arabia and Kuwait. They also include generous commercial credits and loans from the

USA, USSR, Japan, Britain and other Western European countries.[6]

Elaine Sciolino also exposed Saddam's financial crisis at the end of the war with Iran.

> To continue its war with Iran, Iraq had relied on roughly $40 billion in interest-free "loans" and grants from the rich Gulf states—which it expected to be forgiven. Iraq also owed as much as $35 billion to Europe, Japan, and the United States in loans that it would have to pay back in increasingly scarce hard currency, and about $7 billion to $8 billion to the Soviet bloc.[7]

Events leading up to the invasion of Kuwait revealed an escalating debt problem for Saddam's Iraq. Sciolino continues,

> Iraq emerged from the war with Iran with $80 billion in debts—about one and a half times its gross national product. Debt-service payments to foreign creditors alone totaled $6 to $7 billion annually. By the end of 1988, Iraq's cash-flow problem became so serious that it defaulted on loan payments to the United States, Canada, Australia, and Britain. Western banks began to turn down Iraqi requests for credit. ...By the time Saddam invaded Kuwait, according to international bankers, Iraq owed Western creditors $10 billion more than at the end of the Iran-Iraq war.[8]

At least part of the impetus for Saddam to invade Kuwait, then, was that he desperately needed Kuwait's assets. Kuwait is one of the wealthiest Arab nations with huge oil reserves and tremendous investment capital. Saddam needed Kuwait as a means of paying his debts.

Now all of this may seem unrelated and distant from Habakkuk, but as I continued reading in Chapter 2, a further prophecy leaped off the page. Could Habakkuk be referring to Saddam's outrageous indebtedness in these verses?

> **6** Shall not all these take up their taunt against him, with scoffing and riddles for him, and say, "Woe to him who heaps up what is not his own—for how long?— and loads himself with pledges!"
> **7** Will not your debtors suddenly arise, and those awake who will make you tremble? Then you will be spoil for them.
> **8** Because you have plundered many nations, all the remnant of the peoples shall plunder you, for the blood of man and violence to the earth, to cities and all who dwell in them.

Here was another prophecy of Habakkuk against the Chaldeans that had a curious similarity to twentieth century Iraq. It certainly intrigued me. Yet, obvious questions arose. *How much of this is mere coincidence? And, could the same prophecies be accounted for in the events surrounding the rise of the Neo-Babylonian Empire at the end of the seventh century BC?* Investigating that possibility would be the next step in determining the true intent of Habakkuk's prophecy.

SERIOUS REFLECTIONS ON HABAKKUK

Sensationalism sells. *The National Enquirer* and other tabloid publications know that and exploit the public's hunger for the spectacular. **"ANCIENT PROPHET PREDICTS SADDAM'S CRAZY EXPLOITS"** would fit right in as a headline attention-grabber to those standing in line at the supermarket.

But it takes more than coincidence to account for biblical prophecy. Just because modern events have a certain similarity to prophetic predictions doesn't necessarily mean that they are an actual fulfillment of those predictions.

Modern clairvoyants from Nostradamus to Edgar Cayce have thrived on apparent fulfillments of nebulous predictions. The biblical prophets were more precise, however, and a careful study of the prophets' intent and the historical context of their prophetic utterances are the means of weeding out the merely sensational from the truly phenomenal. Habakkuk's prophecy deserves that kind of careful attention.

First of all, it is obvious that Habakkuk wrote to address a current problem. The nation of Judah, of which he was a part, had woefully disobeyed God and had become a serious disappointment compared to what God had called them to be. In the early verses of his writing, therefore, Habakkuk pleaded with God to do something about this national dilemma. There is no question about the fact that Habakkuk's request and God's prophetic decree are connected. The prophecies are intended to be the fulfillment of Habakkuk's request.

In the *second* place, Habakkuk is distraught about what God intends to do. The brunt of the prophecy in Habakkuk is against Israel, not against the nations in general. In other words, the Chaldeans were being raised up by God to invade and capture Israel. Now, Saddam Hussein would have loved to ravage Israel during the Gulf War, but the most he could muster was to lob a few Scud missiles at Tel Aviv.

Saddam's frustrated attempts at empire-building were not the "burden" of Habakkuk. He is aghast at the idea that the Chaldeans would be causing serious harm to Israel—(not plundering Iran and Kuwait). The historical context is very specific and Saddam Hussein's exploits before and during the Gulf War don't qualify as an application of Habakkuk's thoughts.

Thirdly, Habakkuk speaks of the Chaldeans as being successful in their evil endeavors as they plunder and ravage other nations. This in no way describes Saddam Hussein's regime in the twentieth century. Saddam killed a lot of Iranians, but he was not successful in conquering Iran.

When the war with Iran was over, the 750-mile border between the two countries remained essentially the same as it had been. Then as Saddam invaded Kuwait, a mere five months passed before the coalition forces caused him to retreat back to his own border. As we saw in the last chapter, Saddam had evil designs against Saudi Arabia, but that never materialized. With all of his conniving and planning, he could never bring his imperial dream to fruition. In retrospect, this is not the Chaldea Habakkuk was describing.

Consider a *fourth* observation. Some may appeal to the Near View/Far View principle of biblical prophecy and claim that some of Habakkuk's prophecies were fulfilled in the Near View of Nebuchadnezzar, and perhaps others in the Far View of Saddam Hussein. We will see this principle operative in Isaiah's prophecy concerning Babylon in the next chapter of this book, but there is nothing in Habakkuk's prophecy that was not fulfilled in the days of the Neo-Babylonian Empire.

In order for a Far View aspect to be present in any particular prophecy, there is usually an apocalyptic element that is not fulfilled in the contemporary scene, but which points to some future event. Nothing like this is found in Habakkuk's prophecy. Everything can be explained in terms of what the ancient Chaldeans did in the late seventh and early sixth centuries BC. One can find obvious similarities in this prophecy to Saddam Hussein's exploits, as I have pointed out, but they do not appear to be the actual fulfillment of some Far View intent.

THE ANCIENT FULFILLMENT

Habakkuk is not describing history—he is prophesying it. The Chaldeans had not yet invaded Judah in 615 BC, but they were already recognized as an ascending power. They then conquered Nineveh (612 BC) and replaced the Assyrians as the ruling force in Mesopotamia. Yet God is informing Habakkuk that the Chaldeans will soon come against Judah as God's means of chastising His errant people. The prophecy is therefore imminent, but not immediate. Habakkuk knows that the Chaldean invasion is not too far in the future.

As Habakkuk begins to write, a key phrase in his early verses sets the stage for what God is saying. God tells Habakkuk, "Look among the nations, and see; wonder and be astounded. For I am doing a work **in your days**" (Hab. 1:5 – emphasis mine).

God spoke very specifically about when the fulfillment of the prophecy would take place. It would happen in the lifetime of the prophet.

His reference was to the Chaldeans of Nebuchadnezzar's Empire, not a futuristic time in the twentieth century. It would happen "in your days."

So, did all of these things happen in Habakkuk's days? A brief review of the history of Babylon's victory over Judah and the subsequent captivity of the Jews by Nebuchadnezzar's Chaldeans reveals that all Habakkuk foretold *did* come to pass in those days. The book of Habakkuk is a prophecy completely fulfilled in ancient times.

The Chaldeans were indeed "dreaded and feared" (1:7 - NAS) and their horses sped "swifter than leopards" and were "more fierce than . . . wolves" (1:8). As they moved through the land, they scoffed at kings and laughed at rulers (1:10). A powerful force, they swept through "like the wind" (1:11), and fortresses were no match for their engineering skills—as they "heap[ed] up rubble to capture" them (1:10 - NAS).

In every respect, the poetic imagery of Habakkuk's prophecy is fitting to the Chaldean military operations and the conquering exploits of Nebuchadnezzar.

George Rawlinson's words graphically describe the awesome power of this Chaldean force.

> The Babylonian armies were made up of vast hosts, composed not only of native troops, but also contingents from subject nations. They marched with great noise and tumult, spreading themselves far and wide over the countryside, plundering and destroying on all sides. Often they engaged their enemy in pitched battles, but generally they laid siege to the fortress cities of the enemy who had fled behind such defenses. These were assaulted with battering rams and by raising siege-mounds of dirt which would reach nearly to the tops of the walls of the city.[9]

There is no question but that Habakkuk spoke of what was happening in his own day. No aspect of his prophecy has an apocalyptic or far-reaching element extending to the last days of human history. All can be explained quite reasonably from the events surrounding Nebuchadnezzar's invasion of Judah in the closing years of the seventh century BC.

Habakkuk's prophecy was fulfilled in ancient times. It is not a prophecy of the Gulf War and the contemporary madman of Baghdad.

A FINAL WORD

Perhaps in the final analysis all of this study is not wasted effort. True, we have not substantiated our initial thought that this ancient prophet was speaking to our day. Other biblical prophets do speak of our times and they predict events that will transpire at the end of the age—including certain events in modern Iraq.

Yet, there may be one more thing that can be said of all this. There is no doubt that Saddam Hussein aspired to be the Neo-Nebuchadnezzar—a contemporary version of the ancient monarch. In a sense Nebuchadnezzar was Saddam's spirit-mentor. The Chaldean king of old was Saddam's alter-ego. He wanted to think like him, act like him, and even look like him. Above all, Saddam wanted to match Nebuchadnezzar's accomplishments and establish a third Babylonian Empire—a Neo-Neo-Babylonian Kingdom.

So, it should not surprise us that we can find so many similarities between what happened in Habakkuk's day and what happened in the twentieth and twenty-first centuries. In a sense, the Gulf Wars were déjà vu—a mirror image of history past.

As we now know, it was a flawed reenactment, for while Nebuchadnezzar achieved great success, Saddam Hussein achieved deplorable failure. In the end, Saddam was merely an actor playing a part; and when everything was over, the world knew that he was not really Nebuchadnezzar. He was just a poor actor named Saddam Hussein.

That is undoubtedly why certain similarities can be seen between Saddam Hussein's actions and what Habakkuk predicted. That was not the intent of the prophecies, though, and they should not be interpreted accordingly.

At first glance Habakkuk appears to be a prophecy of twentieth century Kuwait, but that is not so. Habakkuk is simply the ghost of Kuwait. Many thought they saw Habakkuk in the events of 1990, but in reality, he wasn't there.

Dan Hayden

Chapter Six

BABYLON: CITY OF DESTINY

Down, But not Out

It was a day like any other day for most of the inhabitants of the favored cities of the southern plain except for six scurrying figures making their way hurriedly to the outskirts of town. The two angels seemed to almost drag their four reluctant companions as they cleared the city limits and headed toward the mountains.

Suddenly a searing bolt of lightning split the cloudless sky and, with laser accuracy, disintegrated the city hall of Sodom. Another followed almost simultaneously, and then another as the heavens swelled with fury. The torments of divine wrath seemed to have gathered in the sky as fiery stones hailed upon the cities of sin, and in less than an hour only the smoldering embers of a once-thriving culture lifted billows of smoke into the air.

It had been a nuclear nightmare engineered in the royal war chamber of a wrathful God. Never before had judgment been meted out in this fashion, and only once more would it happen again—at Babylon.

> And Babylon, the glory of kingdoms, the splendor and pomp of the Chaldeans, **will be like Sodom and Gomorrah when God overthrew them** (Isaiah 13:19 – emphasis mine).

> "For this reason her plagues will come in a single day, death and mourning and famine, and she will be burned up with fire; for mighty is the Lord God who has judged her.

...Alas! Alas! You great city, you mighty city, Babylon!
For in **a single hour** your judgment has come" (Rev. 18:8,
10 – emphasis mine).

Nowhere in the history of ancient times did this infamous city on the
Euphrates River ever experience the type of destruction promised by God.
Bible students therefore must either spiritualize this prophecy, making it
merely symbolic of a military destruction, or look to the future for a literal
fulfillment. While some have opted for the former approach, many are
now seriously considering the latter.

SO, WE WERE WRONG

God has bound Himself by the truthfulness of His Word, but He is not
limited to our faulty understandings and interpretations. A careful
observation of the biblical text and a willingness to let Scripture speak for
itself are indispensable ingredients for an accurate exposition of the Bible.
The prophecies concerning Babylon are impeccable! Unfortunately, our
interpretations of them have often been considerably less than that.

After Isaiah refers to the destruction of Babylon (Isaiah 13:19), he
declares that it will "never be inhabited" (Isa. 13:20) and that "wild
animals will lie down there" (Isa. 13:21).

For approximately two millennia the site of ancient Babylon laid
waste, a fact that led many scholars to assume that the consequences of
God's judgment had been satisfied. Desolate sand-swept ruins were all
that greeted the first team of modern archaeologists in 1899, and apart
from their investigative digging, nothing much had changed since the
fourth century AD when Jerome reported that the whole area was barren.[1]

It seemed obvious. Many commentators were in agreement: The
prophecies concerning Babylon had been fulfilled.

The ruins of Babylon recently uncovered by
archaeologists show how completely the prophet's words
have been fulfilled. ...God has decreed that Babylon shall
never rise again.[2]

Neither will she be inhabited from generation to generation. How truly this prophecy has been fulfilled![3]

Then in 1978 Saddam Hussein began a vigorous program of rebuilding Babylon and a dozen years later it became a reality. Babylon was rebuilt. True, it seemed to be more of "a tourist attraction—a kind of megalomaniacal Disneyland"[4]—than a thriving metropolis; but it is nevertheless a reality in Iraq today.

> Tens of thousands of people are expected at the huge cultural extravaganza planned in Babylon, about 55 miles south of Baghdad.
> The city was rebuilt by President Saddam Hussein at a cost of about $100 million in an ambitious program to revive the splendors of the past and to build a tourist industry following the eight-year Persian Gulf War.
> For two weeks, Babylon's reconstructed palaces and temples will echo with music, opera, dance and drama performed by troupes from the United States, the Soviet Union, Japan and 35 other countries.[5]

So how do we reconcile this with our interpretation that Babylon will never rise again? The answer is we don't. History has simply proven us wrong. We were not as careful as we should have been in our observations of the text of Isaiah.

A LITTLE NEAR-SIGHTED

Isaiah employs an apocalyptic technique often used in the scriptures. Biblical prophets would predict some contemporary event that had an imminent bearing on their audiences, but would also reserve aspects of the prophecies for some future time. Expositors have called this phenomenon the Near View/Far View principle of prophecy. One consequence of this practice is that some texts become rather complicated when the two views (both "near" and "far") are interspersed with each other as though they were one grand prophecy.

In the final analysis, the responsibility of the Bible student is to observe carefully (1) whether or not end-time phrases or descriptions are used, and (2) if any aspects of the prophecy exist which were not fulfilled historically. Generally speaking, these are the major clues indicating that the prophecy contains Far View aspects.

The question for us then is to ask if any futuristic/end-time elements in Isaiah's prophecy concerning the destruction of Babylon can be found. Interestingly enough, there are many! In fact, most of Isaiah's predictions in chapters 13 and 14 seem to be directed toward end-time events.

Isaiah begins his pronouncement of judgment on Babylon by calling upon other nations to rise up against her (Isa. 13:1-5). He refers to "a tumultuous noise of the kingdoms of nations gathered together" (v. 4 - KJV) which is our first indication that something more is contemplated than just the conquering of Babylon by Darius the Mede in 539 BC. Individual nations, and sometimes a limited coalition of a few nations (i.e., the Medes and Persians), had a devastating effect on Babylon at various times over the years, but not until the Gulf Wars has there been anything approaching "kingdoms of nations" arrayed against her.

Phrases like "the day of the LORD" (Isa. 13: 6, 9) and "the wrath of the LORD . . . in the day of his fierce anger" (v. 13) are common notations in the books of the prophets that refer to God's final judgment on the nations prior to the Kingdom Age. Furthermore, descriptive sections mentioning celestial disturbances among the stars, sun, and moon (v. 10) as well as terrestrial upheavals where "the earth will be shaken out of its place" (v. 13) are definitely apocalyptic in nature, having had no fulfillment in the Persian conquest of Babylon.

The flow of Isaiah's prophecy continues as the Kingdom Age of Israel's glory is manifest (Isa. 14:1-8). Isaiah 14:1 demonstrates continuity with the previous section of scripture as Isaiah begins with the word, "For" (Heb. *chi*). This shows a definite relationship to what has just been said. In other words, the result of Babylon's destruction is that Israel will be given rest from Gentile domination (v. 3), and the "whole earth" will enjoy a time of repose from conflict (v. 7).

This certainly did not happen in the days of Babylon's initial destruction, as one kingdom after another (the Persians, the Greeks, the

Romans) sought to usurp control over Israel's welfare. And the earth continues to reel in perpetual conflict over Israel to this very day.

Another interesting aspect of Isaiah's taunt against the fallen monarch of Babylon (14: 9-11) is his mention of Satan's (Lucifer's) fall from heaven (vv. 12-17), where he is "brought down to Sheol, to the far reaches of the pit" (v. 15). According to the Book of Revelation, when Babylon is finally destroyed in the ultimate act of God's judgments against the nations in the Day of the Lord (seventh vial, i.e., bowl – Rev. 16:17-19), the first thing mentioned after Christ's dramatic victory (Rev. 19) is that Satan is bound in "the bottomless pit" (Rev. 20:1-3). Satan and Babylon are linked together intimately from the very beginnings of scripture and Isaiah demonstrates that linkage in the climax of his prophecy of Babylon's ultimate destruction.

It appears then that we have been a little nearsighted in our understanding of Isaiah 13 and 14. We have relegated the destruction of Babylon to the past, and have thereby emphasized the Near View aspect of Isaiah's prophecy. From beginning to end, however, the Far View is predominant; and unless we spiritualize the identity of end-time Babylon (i.e., Rome, the European Union, New York City, etc.), we have yet to see the actual fulfillment of this prophecy.

REBUILT AGAIN AND AGAIN

One of the major fallacies in the previous approach to Isaiah's Babylonian prophecy is the assumption (on the basis of twentieth-century ruins) that Babylon had been totally destroyed "like Sodom and Gomorrah when God overthrew them" (Isaiah 13:19) and that it had never been rebuilt in fulfillment of Isaiah's words that "it will never be inhabited" (v. 20).

The fact that reference is made to "the Medes" (v. 17) gave further impetus to this assumption that it was Darius the Mede who brought Babylon to its end in 539 BC (see Daniel 5:30-31). This Near View part of the prophecy, therefore, became the basis upon which many leaned toward an already completed fulfillment of Isaiah's words.

Darius the Mede, acting on behalf of Cyrus, the Persian (Dan. 6:28), did indeed conquer Babylon. Isaiah was correct when he wrote, in the words of God, "Behold I am stirring up the Medes against them" (Isaiah 13:17). The problem, however, is that Darius didn't destroy the city.

It seems that Gobyrus, one of Darius' generals, devised a plan to divert the waters of the Euphrates, which ran under the walls of Babylon, into lateral canals. This made it possible for Darius' army to slip under the walls and catch the Babylonians by surprise. According to the story, they did this at night while the city was partying with Belshazzar (Daniel 5) so that the Medes conquered the city without firing an arrow. It was a brilliant military move, but more importantly, the city of Babylon was left intact. Thus Isaiah's prophecy was only partially fulfilled.

This seeming inconsistency is recognized by John Martin: "In the Medo-Persian takeover in 539 there was very little change in the city; it was not destroyed . . ."[6] His solution, however, is to assign the prophecy to "the Assyrians' sack of Babylon in December 689 BC"[7] by the Assyrian king, Sennacherib, when extensive destruction was done to the city. The problem with this, as he himself admits, is that Babylon was rebuilt a few years later by Sennacherib's son, Esarhaddon. So, even though Babylon was destroyed a century earlier by the Assyrians, it still did not fulfill Isaiah's words, "It will never be inhabited." Martin tries to duck this problem by adding the phrase, "She will not be inhabited **for a long time**"[8] but even that was not true. Esarhaddon rebuilt the city within a very **short** period of time.

Another attempt at reconciling the apparent inconsistencies of history with Isaiah's prophecy is an appeal to a later destruction of Babylon by the same Medes. Twenty-one years later (517 BC), Darius the Mede (who became Cyrus' successor over the Persian Empire) sought to quell a rebellion against his authority by the same Babylonians, who were more careful about the security of their city this time. Darius was forced to engage a siege of Babylon that lasted for twenty months—a frustrating experience for the Persians, who tried everything to conquer the city without success.

Charles Rollin tells an incredible story as to how the Persians finally defeated the Babylonians.[9] Zopyrus, one of the chief noblemen of the Persian court, mutilated himself (cutting off his nose and ears and inflicting wounds all over his body) as a means of creating a deception with the Babylonians. With Darius' permission, he feigned rejection by the Persians and gained entrance into Babylon as a defector. They, in turn, gave him many favors as a means of obtaining valuable information concerning the Persians' military strategy.

Having received their trust, Zopyrus betrayed the Babylonians by opening the gates, giving Darius entrance to the city. After almost two years of Babylonian mockery, the Persians proceeded to vent their anger as Darius "ordered the gates to be pulled down, and all the walls of that proud city to be entirely demolished."[10]

This second incident against Babylon by the Medes was indeed more destructive than the first. There are several problems, however, in connection with Isaiah's prophecy. For instance, the city was not totally destroyed—only the walls; also, it continued to be inhabited as Darius "contented himself with causing three thousand of those who were principally concerned in the revolt to be impaled, and granted a pardon to all the rest."[11]

The crucial thing to understand is that Babylon never was destroyed in the manner of Sodom and Gomorrah, and each time it was damaged by an invading army, someone came along to rebuild it again.

When Alexander the Great, the Greek conqueror, entered Babylon in 331 BC, it was a thriving city with all of its walls having been rebuilt. The city surrendered peacefully and Alexander proclaimed himself King of Babylon after which he spent ten years reconstructing the Temple of Marduk, Babylon's principal temple. At the age of 32 Alexander the Great died in Babylon (323 BC), and his friend Seleucus Nicator began to rule the city in his stead. In 305 BC Seleucus founded a new capital, Seleucia, forty miles north on the Tigris River (the beginning of Baghdad) and Babylon began to decline as an important center. People continued to live in and around the Babylon area however, until eventually the city was totally abandoned in the early centuries AD. Only then did it begin to fade into the desert sand.

Over the centuries Babylon was rebuilt again and again. Saddam Hussein was simply the latest in a long chain of reconstructionists. The full extent of Isaiah's prophecy has yet to be fulfilled. In his concluding remarks on Babylon's infamous history, historian James Wellard said:

Babylon did not die in a cataclysm as the prophets had hoped, consumed like Sodom and Gomorrah by fire and brimstone, but simply faded away like so many great and beautiful cities of the Middle East.[12]

BACK TO THE FUTURE

Why is Babylon being rebuilt again? Are we making much ado about nothing, or is there prophetic significance to what is currently happening in Iraq?

First of all, make no mistake about it—the city of Babylon has been rebuilt. Charles Dyer makes these observations:

> As of February 1990, over sixty million bricks had been laid in the reconstruction of Nebuchadnezzar's fabled city. Saddam Hussein has ignored the objections of archaeologists who consider it a crime to build over ancient ruins. He has scrapped a plan to rebuild Babylon on a nearby site across the Euphrates River. On the exact site of ancient Babylon, he has reconstructed the Southern Palace of Nebuchadnezzar, including the Procession Street, a Greek theater, many temples, what was once Nebuchadnezzar's throne room, and a half-scale model of the Ishtar Gate.
>
> Hussein plans to rebuild the hanging gardens,...and the ziggurat, or "tower of Babel."[13]

What will become of Saddam Hussein's plans for the future development of this city in the aftermath of the Gulf Wars remains to be seen. To this point there have been no reports of damage to the Babylon area coming out of the wars. Evidently the coalition forces were careful not to bomb sites of archaeological importance. Now that the wars are diminishing, look for a renewal of interest in furthering the Babylon project.

Secondly, Babylon has to be rebuilt at least one more time for the prophecy of Isaiah to be literally fulfilled. As Charles Dyer points out,

"The events concerning Babylon described in the thirteenth and fourteenth chapters of Isaiah were *not* fulfilled in Isaiah's lifetime. They have never been fulfilled."[14]

Prophetically speaking, many things are being revived as we approach the end of the age. The nation of Israel is a modern miracle of national resurrection. Also, most of the nations in the Arab world have found their modern identity in the post-war developments of World Wars I and II. Europe is once again vying for ascendancy on the world scene in what could become a truly remarkable revival of the Old Roman Empire. Furthermore, as we contemplate the amazing changes that have taken place in Eastern Europe and Russia, nothing now seems impossible.

Will the city of Babylon regain a religious and economic importance in world affairs as Revelation 17-18 seem to indicate? Up until now, many have spiritualized "Babylon" to mean Rome or Europe, but since we don't spiritualize the prophecies of Isaiah against other nations, why should we do so with Babylon? We seem to be experiencing an age of revivals—so why not Babylon, too?

The Western World is responding to Iraq after the Iraqi Freedom War as it did to Germany and Japan after the Second World War. As a result, Babylon could become an economic giant in a few short years just as those two countries did. Not having to worry about a military budget after those wars, those countries were able to commit all their resources to economic recovery. It seems that Iraq will be able to do the same.

In light of this, the idea of a revived Babylon could once again become a popular notion, especially as a source of revenue. After all, even Saddam Hussein was able to galvanize international participation with regard to his Babylonian Festival celebrations.

Thirdly, according to Isaiah, the actual destruction of Babylon will come in two stages. Initially an uprising against Babylon by the nations of the world will take place (Isa. 13:1-5). Could the recent Gulf War be the fulfillment of this? Not really. Jeremiah tells us that this coalition of nations will come "from the north" (Jer. 50:9, 41). The entire Gulf War operation by the Desert Storm and Iraqi Freedom multinational forces was from the south. Evidently another military action against Babylon will emanate, not from the southern direction of the Arabian Peninsula, but from the north.

> This group is identified in Isaiah 13:17 as "the Medes." ...Jeremiah confirms that the Medes will be a part of the group to attack Babylon (Jer. 51:11, 28). Who are these Medes? ...The Medes were a people who occupied the mountainous area of northwestern Iran and northeastern Iraq. This is the area occupied by the Kurdish people today. They have been fighting Turkey, Iran, and Iraq in an attempt to establish their own independent country of Kurdistan. Saddam Hussein killed hundreds of their women and children in 1987 and 1988 with poison gas; the hatred of the Kurdish people toward the government of Iraq parallels the hatred of the Medes for the Babylonians described by the prophet Isaiah. The Kurds will take their revenge on the women and children of Babylon.[15]

The second stage of Babylon's destruction will come from God. Actually, this stage may be incorporated into the destruction of Babylon by the nations. There appears to be a direct intervention of divine destruction as the seventh bowl of God's wrath is poured out upon the earth in which "great Babylon came in remembrance before God, to give unto her the cup of the wine of the fierceness of his wrath" (Rev. 16:19 - KJV).

This bowl judgment includes hail out of heaven (Rev. 16:21) which is certainly reminiscent of the destruction of Sodom and Gomorrah with fire and brimstone. At any rate, this combination of invading armies and wrath from heaven will be the final decimation of Babylon, fulfilling literally the words of Isaiah, "like Sodom and Gomorrah when God overthrew them" (Isa. 13:19).

Fourthly, Isaiah tells us when all of this will take place. He says it will happen in "the day of the LORD" (Isa. 13:6, 9). At the very end of the age, just prior to the coming of Christ to establish His Kingdom on earth, Babylon will be destroyed. According to Revelation 16:17-21 this will happen as a part of the seventh vial judgment—the final judgment of all God's judgments in the day of the Lord.

Isaiah's prophecy will be fulfilled in the end of the age. The final fall of Babylon is the symbol of the termination of man's organized system of rebellion against God. In its place, Jerusalem will be exalted as the symbol of Christ's righteous reign upon the earth.

THERE'S STILL MORE TO BABYLON

The term "Babylon" was used in antiquity to refer to the Babylonian Empire of Hammurabi and the neo-Babylonian Empire of Nebuchadnezzar, as well as the city by that name on the Euphrates River. In Chapter Four of this book we noticed that the empire status of Babylon is gone forever in spite of Saddam Hussein's attempt to revive it. In this chapter, on the other hand, we have considered the probability that the city of Babylon will emerge once again as a commercial center of some importance in the reconstruction of modern Iraq. This seems to be the clear indication of biblical prophecy.

That is not all that can be said about Babylon, however. The term is also used to describe the false spiritual system that has permeated the world since the days of creation. This Babylonianism is not restricted to a place and age, but like the proverbial chameleon, it readily changes to fit its background and time.

As we have seen (Chapter Three), it was in Babylon that Satan began his nefarious work of corrupting the world, and from that polluted source every perverted spiritual system has found its way into the cultural niches of the world. The spirit of Babylonianism is alive and well on Planet Earth, and the Bible indicates that the New Age religious unity will find its way back to Mother Babylon.

This, then, is our next subject as we journey back to ancient Babylon in Iraq to trace the twisted trail of the serpent through the ages. It's another fascinating aspect of discovering what the Bible says about Iraq.

Chapter Seven

TOUCHSTONE OF RELIGION
The Harlot and Her Children

All of the religions of the world carry a common designer label—"Made in Babylon." The various fabrics of religious thought and the unique styles of sacramental worship found among the different cultures of the world are the creative work of a single mastermind. According to the Bible, Lucifer, the son of the morning (Isa. 14:12 - KJV) is the genius behind them all—and Babylon on the Euphrates was his workshop.

THE MOTHER-CHILD CULT

Escarbel, high priest in the kingdom of Babylon, stood hesitatingly before the queen, wife of the now-dead Nimrod. He was deeply concerned over the fact that the "succession of rule" issue had not been clearly resolved; that, in turn, was creating an anxious mood in the kingdom. Semiramis, Nimrod's wife, had been the real political genius behind the charismatic leadership of her warrior husband, and Escarbel along with everyone else had been waiting for her to make an authoritative statement concerning who would take his place as chief of the river cities.

Trying hard not to show his impatience, Escarbel finally spoke. "Nimrod, the great hunter and our benevolent chief, has been dead for many months, O Queen, and the people are now looking for direction from you. They are becoming restless. What shall we tell them? What will you do?"

Semiramis smiled, a look of satisfaction and triumph beaming on her heavily painted face. "The Great Spirit has been making his wishes known to me, O son of Belus, high priest of Babel. His plan is ingenious, taken from the old story in the stars."

"Wonderful!" the aged priest exclaimed, "Our great tower of worship is now complete and it will serve us well to tie the governmental structure of our state to the glorious worship of Bel. Our tower reaches into the very heavens, and so it is good that our direction should come from the stars. Please tell me—what is his plan?"

The young queen placed her slender hands on the protruding form of her stomach and slowly raised her head, fastening her dark, penetrating eyes on the old man in front of her. "We will tell the people," she began authoritatively, "that the life now throbbing within my womb was conceived in the heavens and is none other than Nimrod himself returning to life. The child's name shall be Tammuz—a virgin-born son who shall be their guardian and shepherd. The real authority shall rest with me, however. I shall be known as the Virgin Mother, Queen of Heaven and Earth. I am Virgo—the first lady of the stars."

It was done! Perhaps not in the exact fashion as the above vignette, for history is unclear as to how it happened. Semiramis did emerge as the "queen of heaven" (Jer. 7:18; 44:17-19, 25), however, and the mother-child cult was born through her in Babylon. Politics and religion had been wedded into a powerful system of world control.

God in His plan for the ages was not ready for them to succeed, however; so He scattered the people to every curve of the globe by confounding their language. As they went, the new religion went with them under the guise of their new speech. One day they would return, though—at the end of the age.

THE FOUNTAINHEAD

Babylon's identity as the source of the various religious structures of the world has been substantially documented by Alexander Hislop in his classic work, *The Two Babylons*. After examining the numerous linguistic and historical evidences of the origin of religious thought, he makes the following statements:

> If we thus have evidence that Egypt and Greece
> derived their religion **from Babylon,**[1] we have equal

evidence that the religious system of the Phenicians came from the **same source**.[2]

Taking, then, the admitted unity and **Babylonian character** of the ancient Mysteries of Egypt, Greece, Phenicia, and Rome,...[3]

From Babylon, this worship of the Mother and Child spread to the ends of the earth. In Egypt, the Mother and the Child were worshipped under the names of Isis and Osiris. In India, even to this day, as Isi and Iswara; in Asia, as Cybele and Deoius; in Pagan Rome, as Fortuna and Jupiter-puer, or Jupiter, the boy; in Greece, as Ceres, the Great Mother, with the babe at her breast, or as Irene, the goddess of Peace, with the boy Plutus in her arms; and even in Thibet, in China, and Japan, the Jesuit missionaries were astonished to find the counterpart of Madonna and her child as devoutly worshipped as in Papal Rome itself; Shing Moo, the Holy Mother in China, being represented with a child in her arms, and a *glory* around her, exactly as if a Roman Catholic artist had been employed to set her up.[4]

All of this should be no surprise to the student of the scriptures who understands the existence of a satanic conspiracy in the world to undermine and thwart the true gospel of the virgin-born Savior. Satan is the "god of this world" (2 Cor. 4:4) and "the prince of the power of the air" (Eph. 2:2). The Bible teaches that he is in full control of the entire counterfeit system. He is the supreme architect of all demonic doctrines and the foremost administrator of every seducing spirit (1 Tim. 4:1). Religious deception, even in the name of Jesus (2 Cor. 11:13-15) is his specialty, and he is the grand master of spiritual illusion. You can be sure that nothing in the dark world of spiritual perversion happens without his sanction.

The Bible reveals that Satan's nefarious work in the world actually began in Babylon. The Garden of Eden in southern Mesopotamia was his point of entry, but his original attempts at apostasy were demolished in the great flood. Then as opportunity permitted, he began again; and once more Babylon was his center of operation (Gen. 10-11).

BEGINNING OF THE MOTHER-CHILD CULT

The Tower of Babel in Babylon served as both a center of worship and a symbol of unity. The driving force behind this attempt to unify the efforts of man in opposition to God lay in the rebellious minds of Cush, the grandson of Noah, and Nimrod his son. Their plan of bonding together the city states of southern Mesopotamia under a single leadership appears to have been solidified by establishing a religious high place—a tower— for the worship of their contrived deity.[5]

In the Genesis account we read that the tower had a top that reached into "the heavens" (Gen. 11:4). Literally, the text says *whose top in the heavens*. Now, this probably means that it was simply a very high tower reaching up to the sky, but it could also imply that the heavens were the source or object of their worship.

In fact, the works of Joseph Seiss and E.W. Bullinger[6] show that it is almost certain that God had arranged the stars (with their names and configurations) to tell the story of His plan to redeem mankind from its sinful condition. Hundreds of years later God would inscripturate this heavenly plan in a book, beginning with Moses and ending with the fulfillment of His plan in the person of Jesus Christ. For the patriarchs of the pre- and post-flood eras, however, this message was in the stars. Since then the message in the stars has been replaced by the more articulate message in the book we call the Bible.

The 12 signs and 36 decans of the zodiac are an interesting historical study. Satan has perverted God's arrangement of the stars into an alien, occult practice for his own purposes, but the original design appears to have been a divinely created spiritual message in the heavens. Actually, Joseph Seiss points out that the universally accepted pictures of the star groups in the zodiac go back beyond recorded history.

Somewhere in the earliest ages of human existence the stars were named and arranged into groups by some one thoroughly familiar with the great facts of astronomy. Those names and groupings were at the same time included in certain *figures*, natural or imaginary, but intensely symbolic and significant. These names and figures have thence been perpetuated in all the astronomic records of all the ages and nations since. They are founded on indisputable astronomic truth, and hence form the groundwork of all maps and designations of the celestial presentations. They are in all the planispheres, celestial globes, and star-charts among all people, from one end of the earth to the other. Astronomers growl at them, consider them arbitrary and unnatural, and sometimes denounce them as cumbrous, puerile, and confusing, but have never been able to brush them off, or to substitute anything better or more convenient in their place. They are part of the common and universal language of astronomical science. They have place and representation in all the almanacs of all enlightened peoples. They are in all the books and records devoted to descriptions of the heavens. Faith and skepticism, piety and irreligion, alike adopt and use them. Revelation and pagan superstition both recognize them. Heathen, Mohammedans, and Christians, the old with the latest, disagreeing in so many things, yet agree in adopting and honoring these primitive notations of the stars. Even those who have the most fault to find with them still employ them, and cannot get on without them. **And in and from these the showing is, that all the great doctrines of the Christian faith were known, believed, cherished, and recorded from the earliest generations of our race, proving that God has spoken to man, and verily given him a revelation of truths and hopes precisely as written in our Scriptures, and so fondly cherished by all Christian believers.**[7]

If we begin with Virgo (the virgin with a child) as a starting point and work our way around the zodiac to Leo (the ruling lion), we find a striking resemblance to the story of the biblical gospel. When the psalmist says, "The heavens declare the glory of God" (Psalm 19:1), perhaps he is saying more than that the stars are beautiful.

Now the point in all of this is to offer an explanation for the seemingly bizarre notion of Queen Semiramis (wife of Nimrod) that her son Tammuz was "God incarnate" and that he was virgin conceived. Apparently taking the idea from the constellation and decans of Virgo, she presented herself as the embodiment of the divine story and the fulfillment of God's design for human worship. Yet, instead of the son receiving the preeminence, she focused the emphasis on herself as the "Queen of Heaven." In this way, she introduced the concept of the sacred feminine into religious thought and popularized the image of the mother with her child as the object of worship.

According to Hislop, this was the historical beginning of perverted religion and false worship; and it centered on the imagery of Virgo. In the Babylonian version, however, the woman (Semiramis) was glorified above her son (Tammuz):

> Now while the mother derived her glory in the first instance from the divine character attributed to the child in her arms, the mother in the long-run practically *eclipsed* the son. ...Now, what in these circumstances might have been expected actually took place. If the child was to be adored, much more the mother. The mother, in point of fact, became the favourite object of worship. To justify this worship, the mother was raised to divinity as well as her son...[8]

The mother-child cult appears to have been foundational to Satan's initial scheme and, as Hislop has indicated, the essential elements of this system went with the scattered peoples to their new locations around the world. Satan is a clever craftsman, however, and it has been to his advantage to vary his original design according to the cultural views of the various ethnic groups. Adding new lines of religious thought to his growing inventory of spiritual deceptions has also served his ultimate purpose of blinding people to the truth.

On the one hand, Satan is an atheist spewing out his venomous thoughts through the twisted mind of a humanist or communist. Then again he is a monotheist serving Allah as a radical Shiite, or worshipping Jehovah as a self-righteous Pharisee. Or perhaps it is to his advantage to be a polytheist Hindu or an animistic Indian in the jungles of Ecuador. Whatever works! The Deceiver epitomizes the philosophy, "the end justifies the means."

The point I am making is that Babylon (either directly or indirectly) is the fountainhead of all religious thought that is contrary to the gospel of God's grace in Jesus Christ. Two formidable lines of evidence support this claim. The first is the spiritual record given to us by God in His Word that Satan has masterminded a single conspiracy against the truth of God (Eph. 6:11-12), and that it began in Babylon (Gen. 10-11). The second is the historical record which has been documented by Hislop in *The Two Babylons*, and which corroborates the biblical account.

ENTER RELIGION

Religion is a complicated subject with many twists and turns in historical variation and cultural adaptation. The variety of creative alternatives seems endless.

Yet, a common denominator woven into the fabric of religious thought distinguishes all religion from biblical spirituality.

Every religion dedicates itself to a works system of human achievement (good deeds and ritual observances) to please the higher power and to obtain the coveted blessing. Biblical spirituality on the other hand is technically not a religion but a relationship with the benevolent God. It recognizes the complete inability of sinful humanity to effect its own salvation and depends totally on the gracious gift of God to provide forgiveness of sins and eternal life through His heavenly plan of redemption.

In religion, each person must work for his or her own standing before the divine presence. In biblical Christianity, however, God takes the initiative to provide for mankind what it could not accomplish for itself.

Religion is based on the hard work of achieving spiritual status whereas biblical Christianity rests on simple faith in what God has already done. The two systems of thought are diametrically opposed to each other.

In the biblical account, this alternative way of thinking was introduced into the human realm by Satan, who misrepresented himself as a creature of enlightenment. Contradicting God's specific directive for simple obedience, Satan in serpent guise suggested to the first woman that God was actually squelching the couple's spiritual potential.

Mustering his most seductive voice, he spoke in syrupy tones. "You will not surely die. For God knows that when you eat of it [the tree of the knowledge of good and evil] your eyes will be opened, and you will be like God, knowing good and evil" (Gen. 3:4-5). This slick lie has been the crux of all religious thought since that time.

Notice what Satan said. First, he suggested that Adam and Eve could not depend on the God of the Bible to be truthful with them. God said they would die, but Satan said that wasn't true—they needed instead to act independently of God because they could achieve more on their own than God was willing to concede. Since they would know "good and evil," they could determine for themselves what was spiritually beneficial.

Second, Satan told them that by their independent efforts, Adam and Eve could unleash their own divinity—"You will be like God." He deceived Eve into thinking that she had the potential within her to achieve divine status. All she needed to do was to recognize the inner light and discover her true self.

Third, the Deceiver led Eve to believe that she could become the spiritual leader of the man in determining their mutual destiny. She could become the savior and release them from the bondage of spiritual oppression. This was the beginning of the idea of the sacred feminine, and it was only a matter of time before Semiramis would popularize the idea into a pervasive religious notion.

So, in the light of Genesis 3, consider what happened in the Garden of Eden as Satan presented his alternate plan to Eve.

1. A works system of human achievement was introduced as the basis of attaining spiritual status.

2. Spiritual enlightenment was offered as something to be realized by simply unleashing the divine potential within the human soul.

3. The sacred feminine was unveiled as the ultimate savior and true object of worship.

These ideas, in various forms and combinations, are the stuff of religion. And they are the antithesis of biblical spirituality.

In the Genesis account, the temptation of Adam and Eve is presented as an antagonistic challenge to God's plan for humanity. It introduced foreign and destructive thoughts into the spiritual perspective of their relationship with God. Hardship, suffering, and death were the consequences, and instead of experiencing personal fellowship with God, mankind became the enemy of God. It was the beginning of religion—and it is the ultimate evil.

God, no longer accepted on His terms, had been redesigned to conform to man's perverted thinking. Eventually, instead of inventing gods and currying divine favor by religious works, mankind resurrected the idea that they could become their own gods. Semiramis simply took it a step further when she offered the world a female deity. The Satanic cycle of religious perversion was complete. And it all started in the Garden of Eden, somewhere south of Baghdad.

MOTHER OF HARLOTS

Babylon has never lost its spiritual significance. Its importance as a religious center diminished over the centuries prior to the time of Christ, but its spiritual significance was never forgotten.

Assyrian Kings

The Assyrian kings who ruled in Nineveh continued to be infatuated with Babylon as a touchstone of their religious heritage. As John Martin points out, "Nineveh was Assyria's capital, but Babylon became the center of its cultural life. Because of this assimilation, the worship of Babylon's god Marduk gained popularity in Assyria."[9] So though they distinguished themselves from the Babylonians politically, the Assyrians nevertheless retained a spiritual affinity with the Babylonian deities.

Alexander the Great

Years later, the spiritual influence of Babylon could still be seen in the events surrounding the death of Alexander the Great. Alexander's military movements in the Middle East had been swift and far-reaching. Suddenly, though, his aggressiveness waned and he settled down to a sedentary existence of anxiety and debauchery—at Babylon.

The Greek conqueror made Babylon his eastern capital and "spent the greater part of his time in such pleasures as that city afforded."[10] The reason for this radical change in behavior was evidently a spiritual omen of ill fate spoken by the priests and astrologers in that ancient city. Apparently he became obsessed with the idea of repairing the temple of Marduk perhaps as a gesture of goodwill to appease the great god of Babylon. According to Charles Rollin, "Alexander was resolved, not only to rebuild it, but even to raise a much more magnificent temple."[11]

The glorious conqueror of the world was afraid and turned to alcohol as a means of controlling his anxiety. Then, four months prior to his thirty-third birthday, Alexander died in Babylon, collapsing at a banquet after drinking heavily. Some thought that he had been poisoned, but as Rollin points out, "the true poison which brought him to his end was wine."[12] Ensnared in the web of Babylon's religious perversions and seductive licentiousness, Alexander, one of the greatest conquerors the world has ever known, was emasculated and destroyed.

Napoleon

But Alexander wasn't the only conqueror infatuated with Babylon. Anyone with a sense of history and a global perspective understands the strategic importance of Babylon as the juncture between East and West. As a potential world conqueror, Napoleon knew this. Napoleon's ambition was "to conquer the whole of Europe and Asia, and he recognized to that end the strategical position of ancient Babylon as a governmental and commercial centre."[13]

It seems that Napoleon also had plans to rebuild Babylon.

> In the Department of War of France, at Paris, there is
> to be seen the records of valuable surveys and maps made
> by order of Napoleon I, in Babylonia, and among them is a
> plan for a **New City of Babylon**, thus showing that the vast
> schemes of Napoleon comprehended the **Rebuilding of the
> Ancient City of Babylon**, and the making it his Capital...[14]

So, here's the point: Never underestimate the influence and power
of Mother Babylon.

Alexander felt it—and so did Napoleon.

Jeremiah, the Prophet

During the years in which the Babylonian Empire thrived under the
leadership of Nebuchadnezzar, Jeremiah, the prophet of God, spoke of
the prominence of Babylon as the source of religious perversion.
Scripture tells us of Jeremiah's great prophetic condemnation "against
Babylon" (Jer. 50:1 - KJV):

> Babylon was a golden cup in the LORD'S hand,
> **making all the earth drunken; the nations drank of her
> wine;** therefore the nations went mad (Jer. 51:7).

> And I will punish Bel in Babylon, and take out of his
> mouth what he has swallowed. **The nations shall no longer
> flow to him**; the wall of Babylon has fallen (Jer. 51:44).

Jeremiah was reaffirming the central role played by Babylon in the
development of world religions. First, he said that Babylon is the spiritual
cause of the world's madness because it was Babylon that "made all the
earth drunken." Then he mentioned the reciprocal attitude of the nations as
they flowed together back to Babylon, which is what Jeremiah said God
would let them do "no longer" when he destroyed the city. The harlot's
children would never forget their mother, whom John calls "MYSTERY,

BABYLON THE GREAT, THE MOTHER OF HARLOTS AND
ABOMINATIONS OF THE EARTH" (Rev. 17:5 - KJV).

THE WHOLE STORY IS NOT YET TOLD

Well, that seems to be the way it all began.

Spiritual Babylon did indeed entrench herself as a mother of religious thought. Her cultic children wandered the earth and settled in distant places, but affection for mother appears to have been ingrained in their religious souls, which is why an eventual reunion in Babylon is not exactly a stretch of the imagination.

As the apostle John penned The Revelation of Jesus Christ, with its prophetic fore view of things to come, he anticipated the resurgence of Mother Babylon at the end of the age (Rev. 17, 18). According to John, the city of Babylon will flourish once again with all of its religious trappings and abominable practices. It will be the ultimate celebration of the ecumenical spirit.

So perhaps the whole story is not yet told. A simple twist in the current kaleidoscope of international changes could present an interesting variation on the contemporary religious spectrum.

Suppose, for instance, that the world is finally successful in its attempt to neutralize Iraq, making it accessible again to international interests. And suppose that the one-world religion advocates of New Age thinking are looking for a strategic location in their desire to affect a cooperative religious unity between East and West. Is it not possible, in the light of Babylon's historic past, that it could emerge as the ideal setting to fulfill that need? Perhaps we should not be surprised if just such a thing occurs.

CITY OF THE FUTURE

Well, what would it take for all of this to happen? What could possibly skyrocket a festival theme park on the Euphrates River into world prominence as a religious and commercial center? How could a place where no one currently resides become one of the most significant cities in the world? These are pressing questions that beg for an explanation.

So, turn the page and let's probe the possibilities.

PART II

PEERING
INTO
THE FUTURE

Dan Hayden

Chapter Eight

BABYLON AMONG THE NATIONS

The Resurgence and Popularity of Future Babylon

The first round of an enemy AK-47 slammed into the side of Second Lieutenant Andrew Terrell's Amphibious Assault Vehicle (AAV). The armored convoy of seventy tanks and AAVs of the First Battalion, Fifth Marine Regiment had just passed the apartment complex along Rt. 2 on the edge of Baghdad's city limits. Suddenly at 4:15 a.m. a firestorm of explosive flashes and green tracer rounds enveloped the invading U.S. Marines. As Lt. Carey Cash tells the story, Marines near the front of the line said it "looked like a battle scene out of *Star Wars*."[1]

In the early morning darkness the Marines of Alpha, Bravo, and Charlie Companies instinctively returned fire as they kept moving toward their objective—the Al Azimiyah Presidential Palace in the center of Baghdad. The Iraqis had staged an ambush and American casualties mounted to over forty wounded during the first hour of combat. Yet, the convoy pressed on, understanding the strategic importance of capturing the palace.

Slicing through the resistance, U.S. forces fought significant battles through the streets of Baghdad. Along the way they secured a massive bridge along the Tigris River and seized the Abu Hanifah Mosque, used as a fortress by Saddam's Republican Guard. The morning was filled with ferocious fighting, but by noon the battle for Baghdad was all but over.

Entering the vacated palace in the early afternoon, U.S. Marines commandeered Saddam Hussein's symbol of power. Having been the first coalition forces to cross into Iraq from Kuwait just three weeks earlier, Marines of the First Battalion, Fifth Marine Regiment had now penetrated into the heart of Baghdad.

In less than ten hours (4:00 a.m. to 1:00 p.m., April 10, 2003) Baghdad had fallen and only one American soldier had died in the process. In military terms, that is spectacular.

Now, many will undoubtedly attribute such a victory to the superior power of the American military. Yet, Chaplain Carey Cash, who was there that day, believes that God was very present in all that happened. Referring to the words of Lance Corporal Ortiz as he reflected on what appeared to be a miraculous incident, Lt. Cash wrote that Ortiz stated, "Chaplain, God protected me . . . "[2] Then the Chaplain shared his own observations.

> God had protected him, and all of us. And even those who were injured went on to talk about the awesome hand of God shielding them from greater injury or even death. I heard about mines that should have killed but didn't; RPGs impacting vehicles fully loaded with men and not injuring anyone; bullets raining down around Marines striking everything within an inch of their lives; sandstorms that halted enemy counterattacks and revealed hidden mine fields. There was no question that God had literally reached down from the heavens and raised up a hedge of protection around us...[3]

Some will argue that God has not been in everything that America has done and they are undoubtedly correct. But He was there that day and He used the American military to accomplish His purpose. God is preparing the way for change in Iraq and the speedy fall of Baghdad heralded the winds of divine providence.

It may take awhile, but an international future for Baghdad is now a real possibility. Babylon may yet sit as a queen among the nations.

FROM BAGHDAD TO BABYLON

The Bible describes end-time Babylon in glowing terms, both as a religious center and as an economic hub. In reading Revelation 17 and 18, the reader gets the impression that Babylon is THE place of prominence in the world of the future.

According to the Bible, the Antichrist who comes to power as the supreme ruler of the western world embraces Babylon as the symbol of his global philosophy. In this he is very much like Alexander the Great and Napoleon before him who sought to make Babylon the capital of their eastern empires. Make no mistake about it; Babylon has a mystical influence over the imperial dreams of world conquerors.

Yet Babylon today is only a small tribute to Iraqi culture and gives no impression of the greatness ascribed to it in the Bible. Saddam Hussein restored a few buildings and held two cultural festivals there, but it certainly is not a city by any stretch of the imagination. So granted, it is difficult to envision Babylon as the Bible describes it—a religious, cultural, political, and economic super-city. But if we understand the symbolic significance of Babylon and if we realize the desperate need for such a symbol of unity in our fractured world, it is reasonable to expect that sooner or later the world's attention will once again focus on Babylon.

For now, however, the principal city of Iraq is Baghdad. And for now the world's interest is riveted on Baghdad as the epicenter of the East-West struggle. Soldiers from the West are policing the streets and Islamic fundamentalists from the East are blowing up everything in sight. In essence, Baghdad has emerged as the contemporary symbol of economic and religious conflict.

Babylon, on the other hand, remains neutral. Nothing of significance is currently happening there. Only fifty miles south of Baghdad, Babylon is best remembered in modern times for its multinational festival celebrations. Thus, in a way, the precedent has already been set for perceiving Babylon as a place of global unity. In contrast to Baghdad, Babylon could emerge as the symbolic city of peace and prosperity.

BEYOND RELIGION IN BABYLON

In a spiritual sense, Babylon will represent the religion of the future. As the home of the ecumenical religion of the global community it will be politically correct and enjoy the complete approval of the Antichrist's empire. This religious system is represented in the Bible as a tawdry woman whom the apostle John calls, "MYSTERY, BABYLON THE GREAT, THE MOTHER OF HARLOTS."[4] Furthermore, he describes her as having global influence, for she is "the great whore that sits upon many waters" (or many nations).[5] In fact, John represents her as being both pompous and cruel.

> And the woman was clothed in purple and scarlet, and adorned with gold and precious stones and pearls, having in her hand a gold cup full of abominations and of the unclean things of her immorality, …And I saw the woman drunk with the blood of the saints, and with the blood of the witnesses of Jesus. And when I saw her, I wondered greatly (Rev. 17:4, 6 - NAS).

For a time this woman rides on the beast (Rev. 17:3), who is said to be the Antichrist, and his governmental system. The imagery here is that the Antichrist will tolerate the religious system and allow her to be carried along on the back of his political power. She, in essence, will be the state religion. But that will last for a limited time only.

Blinded by success and influence, the woman seems to be impervious to the Antichrist's real agenda, which is to exalt himself as God and to replace religion with emperor worship. For him, religion is only a means of furthering his political purpose. Initially he encourages a symbiotic relationship because religion helps him to gain influence over the people. But eventually she outlives her usefulness and he simply eliminates her.

Turning his political system into the ultimate religion, the Antichrist will allow his subordinate kings to dismantle the harlot woman. According to John's prophecy the political leaders who serve under the Antichrist "will hate" the harlot (probably because she enjoys too much influence) and "will make her desolate and naked, and will eat her flesh and burn her up with fire." [6] Evidently the Antichrist's desire for emperor worship will be so strong that any religious competition will not be tolerated. Religious pluralism will be a thing of the past.

All of this seems to happen at the midpoint of Daniel's 70th week (remember Chapter 1 in this book) when the Antichrist decides to present himself to the world as "God." Apparently it is then—when the religious system is dismantled—that the woman is replaced by the false prophet of Revelation 13, who persuades the entire world to worship the Antichrist. At that point New Age religion will cease to exist in favor of the supreme deification of the Antichrist. This reminds me of the old limerick:

> There once was a lady from Niger
> Who went for a ride on a tiger.
> They came back from the ride
> With the lady inside,
> And a smile on the face of the tiger.

Religion and politics will no longer be separate entities. The governmental system and its ruler will become the new religion.

COMMERCIAL SUCCESS ON THE EUPHRATES

Zechariah's Prophecy

Even though the religious aspect of the future city of Babylon is finally eliminated by the Antichrist, her commercial interests are encouraged and allowed to thrive under his authority. In this regard an interesting prophecy surfaces in the biblical book of Zechariah. Zechariah was a Hebrew prophet living in Israel after the time of the Babylonian captivity. He began his prophecy by revealing eight night visions he had in the year 519 BC.

The seventh of these visions featured a woman in a basket (Zech. 5:5-11) depicting the future commercial success of Babylon. By the time Zechariah wrote his prophecy Babylon had already been in the hands of the Persians for twenty years. Yet in his vision he saw the woman carried in a basket to the land of Shinar, which is Babylon. The prophecy concludes with these words:

> **9** Then I lifted up my eyes and saw, and behold, two women coming forward! The wind was in their wings. They had wings like the wings of a stork, and they lifted up the basket between earth and heaven.
>
> **10** Then I said to the angel who talked with me, "Where are they taking the basket?"
>
> **11** He said to me, "To the land of Shinar, to build a house for it. And when this is prepared, they will set the basket down there on its base."

When Zechariah said that he saw a basket, he was referring to an ancient basket used for measuring grain. Approximately one bushel in size, the basket often symbolized commerce or economic interests. The woman in the basket, according to Zechariah, was named "Wickedness" (v. 8) and seemed to indicate that the commercial enterprise in view would be characterized by fraud, deceit, and evil profiteering. The fact that the basket is carried to Shinar (Babylon) means that this corrupt but lucrative commercial system will be developed and centered in southern Iraq.

> [T]he basket will be taken to the land of Babylon. After the flood, the first outbreak of evil in the world occurred at Babylon. Everything will come full circle. The world's first capital city will be the place of its final city, Babylon. I believe this means that, in the end times, Babylon will become the world capital of an evil world economic system run by Antichrist.[7]

John's Revelation

What Zechariah anticipated in his vision, the apostle John described almost six hundred years later as he wrote the last chapters of the Book of Revelation. After envisioning the demise of Babylonian religion in chapter 17, John saw "another angel coming down from heaven" (18:1) with a message concerning the destruction of commercial Babylon. The entirety of chapter 18 then is devoted to the angelic pronouncement of doom on this great economic enterprise and the extreme disappointment of merchants and politicians as they contemplate their enormous loss.

1. A Commercial Success

What is surprising about this prophetic revelation concerning end-time Babylon is the global scope of her commercial success. Babylon today exists only as a dramatic theme park (Saddam Hussein's center for folk festivals), used currently by coalition forces as a motor pool base camp. It doesn't even qualify as a small town, let alone a great city.

Yet John wrote confidently that "the merchants of the earth have grown rich from the power of her luxurious living" (Rev. 18:3). Some Bible commentators are even so bold as to suggest that John is predicting that one day Babylon will become "the center of world finance and commerce"[8] replacing New York, London, Paris and Geneva.

Actually John's description of Babylon's commercial interests is very detailed. Twenty-eight categories of items are mentioned in two verses (12 and 13) of Revelation 18, which seem to be representative of the types of things that make for a successful commercial center. In the context of describing Babylon's final destruction, John writes (Revelation 18):

> **11** And the merchants of the earth weep and mourn for her, since no one buys their cargo anymore,
>
> **12** cargo of gold, silver, jewels, pearls, fine linen, purple cloth, silk, scarlet cloth, all kinds of scented wood, all kinds of articles of ivory, all kinds of articles of costly wood, bronze, iron and marble,
>
> **13** cinnamon, spice, incense, myrrh, frankincense, wine, oil, fine flour, wheat, cattle and sheep, horses and chariots, and slaves, that is, human souls.
>
> **14** "The fruit for which your soul longed has gone from you, and all your delicacies and your splendors are lost to you, never to be found again!"

15 The merchants of these wares, who gained wealth from her, will stand far off, in fear of her torment, weeping and mourning aloud,

16 "Alas, alas, for the great city that was clothed in fine linen, in purple and scarlet, adorned with gold, with jewels, and with pearls!

17 For in a single hour all this wealth has been laid waste." And all shipmasters and seafaring men, sailors and all whose trade is on the sea, stood far off

18 and cried out as they saw the smoke of her burning, "What city was like the great city?"

Notice that "the merchants of the earth" (v. 11) trade with her, showing the global nature of her business. Note also that she is called "the great city" (vv. 16, 18), revealing her prominent stature among the nations. As one commentator put it, "The combined picture is one of complete abandonment to the wealth of this world and total disregard of God who gave it."[9] These descriptions of a revived Babylon seem to indicate that a luxurious city of great importance will indeed arise out of the ruins of the once fabulous city of ancient Babylon.

2. International Festivals

One other point of interest is how Babylon will evidently capture the world's attention with music and enticing festivals. The apostle John adds this prediction in chapter 18 of the Book of Revelation:

22 and the sound of harpists and musicians, of flute players and trumpeters, will be heard in you no more, and a craftsman of any craft will be found in you no more, and the sound of the mill will be heard in you no more,

23 and the light of a lamp will shine in you no more, and the voice of bridegroom and bride will be heard in you no more, for your merchants were the great ones of the earth, and all nations were deceived by your sorcery.

What is captivating about this aspect of the prophecy is that Saddam Hussein has already set the precedent for this in his resurrection of Babylon as a festival center. Prior to the Desert Storm War in 1990 Saddam had already held two international festivals in the rebuilt facilities of Babylon. Charles Dyer, an American Bible scholar, attended both of Saddam's festive occasions and wrote of the international interest in these celebrations.

> When I attended the Babylonian Festivals in 1987 and 1988, guests from all over the world gathered there. There were ballet troupes from the Soviet Union and France, opera singers from Italy, folk dancers from Greece, Turkey, Poland, and Yugoslavia, flamenco artists from Spain, a symphony from the Soviet Union, and Bedouin dancers from Saudi Arabia. The Iraqis even invited Madonna, who didn't show.
>
> "This is not just an Iraqi festival," Munir Bashir told a writer for the *Los Angeles Times*. "It is a festival for the whole world, because Babylon was the capital of civilization once and has given the world so much. People from all over the world want to see Babylon. All the time we have requests."[10]

Two wars and over a decade of U.N. sanctions against Iraq have put a halt to these festive events. Yet the initial structures of rebuilt Babylon remain intact and resuming these activities could happen within a very short period of time. Remember the words of Munir Bashir (Iraq's Babylonian Festival organizer), "People from all over the world want to see Babylon."

BABYLON MEANS BABYLON

Now, I grant you that all of this seems to be a bit of a stretch in light of current circumstances in Iraq. Baghdad is the principal city of Iraq, and Babylon is no more than a tourist destination fifty miles south. Major changes would need to take place in order to make the above scenario a reality. Yet, a preponderance of conservative Bible scholars today is suggesting that this is exactly what will happen.

One of the foremost authorities on the biblical perspective of end-time Babylon is Charles Dyer. He has traveled extensively in the Middle East and, as noted above, he attended both of Saddam Hussein's festivals in Babylon. Dyer, having written a doctoral dissertation on the subject, went on to publish two books about the resurgence of Babylon in the light of biblical prophecy.[11] As a result of these pursuits he has come to the conclusion that Babylon will indeed be rebuilt as a religious and commercial symbol for the new globalism that will eventuate in the Antichrist's empire.

> Babylon will be a great city again. The Bible mentions Babylon over two hundred and eighty times, and many of those references are to the future city of Babylon that is rising from the fine sands of the desert today.
>
> ...The time and place have not been right for thousands of years, but when God's prophetic plan is ready, Babylon will be rebuilt. Wickedness will again reign from the plain of Babylon. The city where man's rebellion against God began will be the site where man's rebellion will return to take up residence.[12]

Another contemporary writer on the subject of Babylon's prophetic future agrees with Dyer. In his excellent book *The Second Coming of Babylon*, Mark Hitchcock expresses the same conclusion.

> Based on the evidence, I believe we must conclude that Babylon will rise again. Since these prophecies must be literally fulfilled, they can only be fulfilled if they refer to a future city of Babylon that will be rebuilt and destroyed in the end times.[13]

This is also what I believe the Bible is saying. Somehow conditions will prevail that will lead the world to focus on Babylon as the solution to global barriers. The East-West impasse of ideologies will apparently dissolve as world leaders negotiate the erection of a new center from which all can profit. It will be a neutral site at the juncture where East meets West. And it will have a symbolism that will herald the new globalism of the future.

It really does appear that Baghdad will give way to Babylon, which will become the city of tomorrow.

POSSIBILITIES FOR A PEACEFUL SOLUTION

1. In the Center of it All

Peace is elusive. How many summits and peace accords and shuttle diplomacies and U.N. resolutions and unilateral mini-steps have dotted the Middle East landscape over the past decades? In seeking peace, the West seems to be motivated by economic interests and energy resources, while the East is obviously more bound by its religious traditions.

The United States is currently trying to impose a free market democracy in a region of the world that knows nothing of what that means (apart from Israel), while the Islamic fundamentalists from all over the Middle East are blowing up themselves and others in a warfare of religious ideology. Everybody is losing and yet no one has been able to offer a viable plan to end the violence and bloodshed. Without question, the world is increasingly ready for a solution.

As in any negotiation between truly alienated parties, there must be a meeting of the minds somewhere in the middle. Now, it is not my purpose here to offer a suggestion as to what ought to be done—greater minds than mine have struggled over this seemingly insurmountable problem for years. However, it does seem obvious that compromise and conciliatory efforts will play an important role in any successful peace initiative. Modern Israel understands this as well as anybody.

Since religion (East) and economics (West) are apparently the key ingredients in this stalemate, it would seem to me that a symbol of harmony and unity in these two areas would certainly be an attractive addition to the peace process. This would especially be true if the symbol had ancient significance and global proximity to the contested region.

Babylon certainly fulfills these criteria. As a religious, economic, and political symbol of unity, it is perfect. So is the location.

> Computer studies of the Institute for Creation Research have shown, for example, that Babylon is very near the geographical center of all the earth's land masses. It is within navigable distances of the Persian Gulf and is at the crossroads of the three great continents of Europe, Asia, and Africa.
>
> Thus there is no more ideal location anywhere for a world trade center, a world communications center, a world banking center, a world educational center, or especially, a world capital! The greatest historian of modern times, Arnold Toynbee, used to stress to all his readers and hearers that Babylon would be the best place in the world to build a future world cultural metropolis.[14]

According to the Bible, Babylon has great spiritual significance to Satan and his plan for world domination. The Tower of Babel in Babylon was his initial attempt to galvanize such a plan of global unity. Why would it not be symbolically significant for him to return to Babylon in the culminating age of his Antichrist's world supremacy in order to finish what he started? As you can see, there are many reasons why rebuilding Babylon as a world center is not such a farfetched idea. And Saddam Hussein has already given the idea a head start.

2. City of Seven Hills with a Harbor

Geographically speaking, two reasons stand out as to why literal Babylon has been passed over as the logical choice for this end-time scenario. In Revelation 17, the Bible says that this city will be located in the midst of seven hills (v. 9- NIV)—a description that fits Rome more than Babylon. Additionally, in Revelation 18 we find reference to ships and sailors (vv. 17, 19) implying that this city has a harbor which, apart from its location on the Euphrates River, Babylon does not possess.

So the name Babylon has been viewed by some as a metaphorical idea more than a literal place. Since Alexander Hislop equated the religious aspect of Babylonianism with the Roman Catholic Church,[15] Rome with its seven hills emerged as the choice of many to fulfill these prophecies. On the other hand, as a chief financial hub with a prominent commercial harbor, New York City has been the choice of others. The question is *Can Babylon in Iraq fulfill these two identifying factors?*

City of 7 Hills

First, let's consider the question of seven hills. The woman, who is the ecclesiastical system, is said to sit on these hills. Now, Rome has traditionally been known as the city of seven hills.

> Seven hills formed the nucleus of the ancient city on the left bank of the Tiber. These hills received the names of Palatine, Aventine, Caelian, Esquiline, Viminal, Quirinal, and Capitoline. As Rome grew, however, the hill Janiculum on the other side of the river Tiber was often included among the seven,... Later the hill Pincian to the north of the ancient city was also included in the hills of Rome as the city developed and moved north.[16]

Well, those that have argued for Rome as the apocalyptic Mystery Babylon have emphasized this geographical description and used it as the defining factor.

Babylon on the Euphrates, on the other hand, was not known for any hills, let alone seven. Yet, in recent years hills have emerged in the area of Babylon as a result of Saddam Hussein's reconstruction efforts. Charles Dyer tells us "Three artificial hills, each almost a hundred feet high, have been built on the plain and planted with palm trees and vines."[17] That being true, four more hills could be a reference to a future rebuilt Babylon, rather than a geographical description of historical Babylon.

All of this is a moot argument, however, in that the apostle John tells us that the hills aren't actual hills. In Rev. 17:10 he writes, ". . . and they are seven kings" (NAS). In Scripture, kingdoms are often represented by the term "mountain" (cf. Dan. 2:35, 44-45), which can also refer to the king of that kingdom. The bottom line here then is that the scarlet-colored harlot (the corrupt religious system) is supported by seven kingdoms and their rulers. A rebuilt Babylon therefore is not eliminated by this reference to seven hills.

City with a Harbor

Second, we have to consider the matter of a harbor. Babylon doesn't have a deepwater harbor, but then neither does Rome. Both cities are on rivers and considerably inland from the sea. Well, that's where New York City has come in. The Twin Towers on lower Manhattan were a symbol of commercialism in New York Harbor, which is why they were targeted by terrorists in their symbolic act of destruction. It also is why New York City has sometimes been chosen as the possible Mystery Babylon of end-time events.

Without doubt, a great deal about New York City reflects the ideals of Babylonianism as pictured in the commercial enterprise of Revelation 18. Yet, it seems quite a stretch for the apostle John to be talking about a city so unconnected to ancient times. So much about the biblical record has to be spiritualized to find meaning other than literal meaning, if a modern city like New York is what is meant by the term "Babylon." If we stay with a rebuilt city of Babylon, however, then John can be understood to be saying exactly what he means.

So, what about a harbor for Babylon?

It is no secret that Saddam Hussein wanted a deep sea port, not only for his oil exports, but also to develop a competitive Navy.

> It was unacceptable to Saddam that a country as great as Iraq did not have a long coastline. Over and over he talked about the necessity of building a Navy and becoming a seafaring power. Iraq's isolation from the sea was a cruel accident of history, he believed, and one that had to be rectified—a theme he continued to dwell on after his invasion of Kuwait.[18]

Actually, the Tigris and Euphrates Rivers converge in southern Iraq and enter the Persian Gulf in Iraqi territory. The problem has been that Iran and Kuwait squeeze Iraq into a bottleneck at the mouth of the rivers and Iraq's attempts to forge a harbor there have been thwarted by the hostile refusals of those two countries.

But suppose international pressures were brought to bear upon Iran to allow Iraq access to the Shatt al-Arab waterway all the way to Basra and cooperation could be coerced from Kuwait to open up the area around its little islands of Bubiyan and Warba. A commercial port and harbor for ships could become a reality for Babylon in a relatively short period of time.

Elaine Sciolino described the situation:

> Despite the cease-fire in the Iran-Iraq war, the Shatt remained closed to traffic and Basra was left half-destroyed. The waterway was blocked with years of silt and unexploded mines, and to restore it to working condition would have been a major undertaking. The only way for Iraq to get a port was to dredge the Khor Abdullah channel, the narrow waterway that curved around the Kuwaiti islands of Bubiyan and Warba along Kuwait's coast and led to the Iraqi port and naval base of Umm Qasr. Possession of these islands would also have given Saddam the opportunity to develop a blue-water, or deep-sea, Navy, a goal that had been thwarted by the Iran-Iraq war.[19]

With modern dredging equipment, a deep channel waterway could be opened from the Persian Gulf all the way to Babylon. With its location on the Euphrates River, ships and sailors could indeed have access to this future queen of modern cities. The Antichrist ruler, with his political and economic power and global influence, could easily make that happen. So, as you can see, a harbor in Babylon is not at all out of the question.

HERE'S THE POINT

If we take biblical prophecy at its face value, then we must understand the prophets to mean precisely what they say. This, of course, necessitates taking figurative language and metaphorical expressions to be just that—figures and metaphors. When John said that the seven hills in Revelation 17 were seven kings, then we know that he was using a metaphorical analogy to talk about kings, not hills. But when there is no clear indication of an alternative meaning, we are obliged to read the prophet in a literal sense. References to Babylon in all of the prophets are a case in point: Babylon clearly seems to mean Babylon.

What I am getting at in this section is the real possibility that literal Babylon could very well be the city on seven hills with a harbor. Why go to Rome or New York City when a rebuilt city of Babylon can easily fit the scenario of biblical prophecy? I am suggesting that Isaiah and Jeremiah and Daniel and John meant exactly what they said when they prophesied of a future Babylon with global significance.

Chapter Nine

NOT EXACTLY A MIRACLE

Iraq Could Very Well Have a Prosperous Future

Looking at a 14-acre parcel of land that was nothing more than scattered trees and thick, wild underbrush, I asked my friend what he was thinking.

"This is ideal," he said. "I envision a themed Christian attraction right here that will help people understand the Jewish roots of the Christian faith."

I probed his thoughts even further.

"Well, over there," he said, "I see a towering ancient wall with an entrance gate much like the Jaffa Gate in Old Jerusalem. Then, behind the gate we'll build a 7-story high replica of Herod's Temple with a magnificent courtyard. And over there . . ."

He continued enthusiastically, painting a vivid imaginary picture of an attraction that seemed nothing less than magical. It was all right there—in his mind's eye.

Shortly after our visit to the property, my friend purchased that piece of land—and not long after, what had existed only in his mind had become a reality. He was not a prophet, but he could visualize possibilities in unlikely places. We all know people like that.

When the biblical prophets perceived the future, much of what they described was like the scenario with my friend. They saw special things that transcended what could be seen with the natural eye. When the prophet John spoke of Babylon's future, he saw a magnificent city of international stature rising out of the ancient ruins of old Babylon. And, just because the rest of us can't see it, that doesn't mean it won't become a reality.

What, then, will it take to make all of this happen? Let's engage in some possibility thinking. Starting with Babylon as it exists today, let's combine what we know about political trends and modern technology with the assumption that the Bible is speaking literally—that ancient Babylon will be rebuilt as a religious and commercial global center.

WHAT IT WILL TAKE

1. Eliminate hostilities in the region

War leads to destruction. It is in the atmosphere of peace that we make our greatest strides in cultural advancement and human achievement. If one builds, and another tears down, progress is thwarted and frustration rules. But if everyone works together toward a common goal, great things can happen. That, in essence, is the bottom line with regard to the future of Iraq.

The problem in Iraq has always been warring factions. Whether outside intruders or conflicting ideologies, cultural progress has been limited in Iraq because all energies and resources have been concentrated on warring efforts. Even though Saddam Hussein succeeded in galvanizing the Iraqi people through intimidation and authoritarian rule, he bankrupted the culture with his expansionist exploits and military expenditures. After ten years of war with Iran, no money remained to finish the rebuilding of Babylon.

Now the world is increasingly ready to pour millions (probably billions) of dollars and euros into Iraq's future development. Yet, rebuilding continues to be hindered because Islamic factions cannot give up their warring ways. True, a lot of progress has been made in spite of the insurgents' hateful interference. But, what has been accomplished is nothing compared to what will be possible if peace and freedom can rule in the region.

So, how can that happen? The scholar and military historian Victor Davis Hanson has some advice for us in this regard. He observes, "In wars against bombers and terrorists, the past teaches us that peace comes first through their defeat—not out of negotiations among supposedly well-meaning equals."[1] He then goes on to say,

> It should be our job to find true democrats, both in and outside of the existing governments, and then promote their interests at the expense of both the fundamentalists and the tribal grandees.
>
> ...The contemporary Arab world is like the old Communist domain of Eastern Europe and the Soviet Union, with its political and intellectual tyranny. We should accept that, and then adopt the same unyielding resolve to oppose governments that lie, oppress, and murder—until they totter and fall from their very own corrupt weight. There was a silent majority yearning to be free behind the Iron Curtain, and so we must believe that there is also one now, just as captive, in an unfree Middle East.[2]

If Babylon is ever to become what the Bible indicates it will be, hostilities in the region of Iraq and the surrounding Middle East must be eliminated. When that happens the probabilities for a grand economic and political future for Iraq are boundless. Babylon, as a rebuilt city with global significance, would indeed become a genuine possibility.

2. Initiate a political system that promotes freedom

Political reform and representative government have been the agenda of the U.S. in the post-war efforts in Iraq. From a western perspective, democracy and a free-market economy are the only ways to develop a free society. Yet there are inherent dangers in trying to impose our western thinking on a Middle East culture too quickly.

In her thought-provoking book *World on Fire*, Yale Law School professor Amy Chua argues for a more thoughtful and patient procedure.

> To summarize, there is always an inherent instability in free market democracy. ...Every one of the Western democracies has alleviated the potential conflict between

the rich few and the poor many through a host of devices, past and present, such as extensive social safety nets and redistribution, gradual expansion of the suffrage, upward mobility, and even racism. It is important to recognize, as we export free market democracy to the non-Western world, that many of these stabilizing devices do not exist in the developing world, that some of them are unsavory, and that others are, practically speaking, unreproducible.[3]

My point here is that the goal of creating a free Iraq with economic stability will continue to be a challenge. The fact that Iraqis now have their first democratically elected government is a huge step, but contrary forces throughout the Islamic world continue to raise voices of resistance.

At this stage it may yet seem that we are hoping for the impossible, but remember—in God's timing impossible things do happen. The biblical picture indicates, as we have seen, that Babylon will exist within a free-market society. Whether that includes a democratic form of government remains to be seen, but initial efforts toward a representative government in a very factious country have raised our hopes to the level of "this could actually happen." After all, there is already a model for a democratic free-market society in the Middle East that has been highly successful in spite of its diversified population—and that is Israel.

3. Unleash the oil potential

A major resource to improve the Iraqi economy is oil.

One of the first objectives of the U.S. Marines and coalition forces as they moved into Iraq from Kuwait was to secure and protect the oil fields. Retreating Iraqi forces were under orders to torch the wells as a strategy to prevent their use by the invading enemy, much as they did in Kuwait during the first Gulf War. For the most part, that didn't happen—although the continuing insurgency has tried to destroy the infrastructure of pipelines and wells. Everyone, you see, understands the importance of oil to the future development of Iraq.

The oil and natural gas potential in Iraq is enormous. Second only to Saudi Arabia in the Middle East region, Iraq's oil and gas capacity has only begun to be tapped. According to one report, "Only about 10 percent of the country has been explored. Some analysts . . . believe, for instance, that deep oil-bearing formations located mainly in the vast Western Desert region could yield large additional oil resources."[4]

In that regard, Mark Hitchcock reports that "some believe that Iraq may even have as many as 300 billion barrels, which would then equal about 25 percent of the known reserves in the world"[5] and would propel Iraq ahead of Saudi Arabia as the world's leading producer of oil.

Development of these energy resources will take a little time, but ultimately Iraq has the potential of becoming a very wealthy and prosperous nation. Two problems need to be corrected for that to happen, however. *First*, a more effective security against terrorism and the insurgency needs to be established. Iraq's oil ministry spokesman said in July, 2005 that "there have been 300 acts of sabotage against infrastructure in 2 years," and "70 acts of sabotage took place in the first five months of 2005."[6] All of this has amounted to almost $12 billion in losses. The encouraging news is that the U.S. military has set up "Task Force Shield to guard Iraq's energy infrastructure" and a South African security company is training "6,500 armed guards to protect Iraqi oil wells, pipeline refineries, and power plants."[7]

A *second* concern is the deplorable condition of Iraq's existing wells and facilities. It seems that Saddam Hussein was guilty of over-pumping many wells, which allowed a "damaging intrusion of water into oil reservoirs."[8] Furthermore, in an article titled, "Why Iraq Oil Money Hasn't Fueled Rebuilding," Howard LaFranchi reports that "the state is placing revenue production over maintenance and modernization, . . . risking long-term damage to oil fields."[9] He further quotes Jamal Qureshi, an oil-market analyst, as saying that "perhaps 5 percent of oil revenues are being lost to theft and product smuggling."[10]

So, it's easy to see, much needs to be done to corral the energy resources for productive use in the rebuilding effort in Iraq. As that happens (and a great deal of effort already is being put into making it happen), other projects like the rebuilding of Babylon, will become increasingly possible.

4. Revive the agricultural industry

Iraq has been called "the land of black mud," indicating the rich fertility of its soil. Realistically, it could become the breadbasket of the Middle East. With two rivers flowing through the land, the potential for agricultural greatness is huge. In the past, Nebuchadnezzar's Hanging Gardens was named one of the Seven Wonders of the Ancient World,[11] which symbolized the agricultural genius of the early Babylonians in their development of innovative techniques to harness the water of the Tigris and Euphrates Rivers.

The potential for returning to past supremacy in the realm of agriculture still exists. Early in the twentieth century, Clarence Larkin observed that "the whole country of Mesopotamia, Assyria and Babylonia, only needs a system of irrigation to make it again the most fertile country in the world."[12] The infrastructure of canals and dams has been neglected over the years, but according to Paul Bremer's report of the Ministry of Agriculture's progress as of May, 2004, "In the past year, the Ministry of Agriculture has rehabilitated Iraq's agricultural colleges so that a new generation of Iraqis can carry forward the agricultural history begun here thousands of years ago."[13]

The realization of this potential would mean that Iraq would have another major industry, in addition to oil and gas, from which to grow a prosperous economy. They would not have all of their eggs in one basket, having developed diversity in their economic structure. The biblical significance of end-time Babylon as a hub of agricultural exports would then become a realistic expectation.

5. Develop a harbor with access to the Persian Gulf

An increase in oil and gas exports coupled with a vast array of agricultural products would demand the capacity to distribute those resources to the rest of the world. I have already discussed the idea of a deepwater port for Iraq on the Persian Gulf that would necessitate the cooperation of Iran and Kuwait with Iraq. This is an increasingly possible scenario given the recent agreement between Iraq and Iran to build three pipelines across their southern border in order to exchange "crude oil" from Iraq with "petroleum and refined oil products" from Iran.[14] Iranian

Vice President Mohammad Reza Aref sees this as an opportunity to "recover from decades of frosty relations" and "to become a model of firm ties in the region."[15]

The Tigris and Euphrates Rivers join in their progress to the Gulf just north of Basra. As the convergence of the two rivers flows along the last stretch of 120 miles, it becomes the border between Iraq and Iran until it empties into the Persian Gulf. This section of the river is known as the Arvand River (along the Shatt al-Arab) and is currently "not suitable for navigation because it is covered with piles of mud, wreckage of ships and existence of marine mines."[16]

Nevertheless, the dredging of the Arvand River has become "of utmost priority to Iraq because it links the country to the Persian Gulf."[17] With modern dredging equipment all that is needed are a commitment of resources, international cooperation, and a sense of priority to cut a deepwater channel all the way to Basra. Apparently cooperation and desire are only waiting on the commitment of money to make the project a reality.

Continuing on to Baghdad on the Tigris or Babylon on the Euphrates would only require more time and money. There is no question that the project would be doable if there was a universal desire to have it done. With pressure from the Antichrist to enhance the value of Babylon, such a thing could easily happen.

Think about the incredible success of the Erie Canal connecting the Great Lakes region with the Hudson River and New York Harbor to Buffalo, New York. Taking only eight years to build (1817-1825) the 363-mile canal was subsequently enlarged so that "the system today embraces about 520 miles . . . of waterway and has 57 locks."[18] The genius of this highly successful project was that the canal "became busy with freight and passenger traffic and reaped a good profit."[19] The harbor in New York City was linked successfully with cities on the Great Lakes. Remember, this all began early in the nineteenth century. Just think of what could be done in the twenty-first century.

Could Babylon become a commercial city with a capacity to ship goods to the rest of the world through the Persian Gulf? Sure it could. Nothing is standing in the way of that possible development.

6. Open the country to Tourism

Tourism is one of the pillars of Israel's economy. In addition to the obvious biblical sites that attract people from all over the world, Israel boasts excellent hotels, restaurants, resorts in exotic locations, world-class museums and cultural opportunities. Obviously tourism is down in Israel today due to the Palestinian resistance, but according to BBC News, "About 2 million people a year visited Israel throughout the 1990s, hitting a record of 2.4 million in 2000."[20]

Iraq quite frankly has a similar potential. Many roots of biblical history lie in Iraq, and as for secular history, its ancient sites rival the antiquity of Egypt and the pyramids. When there is a freedom from terrorism and an opportunity to erect five-star hotels, gourmet restaurants and upscale resorts (all operating in a free society catering to tourism), the response will most likely be very favorable.

If the Babylon festivals of the late '80s are any indication of international interest in Babylon, tourism could become a major part of Iraq's economy—much as it is in Israel. People are interested in Babylon and they want to see it.

The head of Iraq's tourism board, Ahmed al-Jabouri, insists that "he has a 'happy heart' when he thinks about the tourism potential of a country that . . . prides itself in being the cradle of civilization."[21] Furthermore, he attests that in spite of the current turmoil in the country that discourages tourism, "his 2,474 staff are keeping themselves busy."[22]

Clearly, an increase in international visitors is on the horizon as soon as Iraq can be stabilized. When that happens, Babylon will again become an important consideration and tourism will make a significant contribution to Iraq's economy.

7. Create a city in a short period of time

When Seleucus Nicator, Alexander the Great's heir in Babylon, began to assess the value of Babylon to his own rule, he decided to create a new city that would bear his name. So, forty miles north of Babylon he founded the city of Seleucia in the vicinity of what we now know as Baghdad. It was the beginning of the decline of Babylon.

As we approach the end of the age, we very likely could see a reversal of that direction initiated by Nicator. In his day, Babylon was an established city with international notoriety. Developing a new city in proximity to Babylon must have raised a lot of eyebrows in that ancient city. Yet Nicator saw it as a strategic move to solidify his rule in the area.

Authority and motivation are all that are needed to make such a change. Today, Baghdad is the recognized city in the center of Iraq and the idea of returning to Babylon is raising a lot of modern eyebrows. Such a thing could happen, though, if an entrepreneurial spirit sees the revival of Babylon as a strategic move in solidifying the authority of the New World Order.

Building a new city in a short period of time is no problem. Modern methods of construction coupled with adequate finances and manpower could establish a city on the Euphrates almost overnight. Clarence Larkin anticipated this.

> It is the purpose of European capitalists to revive the country of Babylonia and rebuild its cities, and when once the time comes the city of Babylon will be rebuilt almost in a night and on a scale of magnificence such as the world has never seen.[23]

As far as the speed of construction is concerned, precedents for rapid building of significant communities can be seen in recent times. In a section titled, "How Quickly Can Babylon Be Rebuilt?" Mark Hitchcock tells the story of Oak Ridge, Tennessee:

> Until 1942, the area where Oak Ridge is located was rural and remote despite being only twenty miles from Knoxville. That all changed dramatically when the government decided to build three facilities there to extract uranium-235 isotopes from uranium ore as part of our country's efforts to build an atom bomb. The Army built a complete city there virtually overnight, with shopping centers, schools, cafeterias, entertainment, a

hospital, a newspaper, and other facilities. Within eighteen months the city had 100,000 residents. A huge bus network was quickly developed to provide transportation for the residents around town, to the three plants, and to Knoxville.[24]

Other stories could be told as well. One, for instance, comes out of the Middle East in the United Arab Emirates near the established city of Dubai. This new phenomenon is known as Dubai Internet City and serves much of the technical needs of the Middle East. While not a mega-city, it is still substantial in size. Hitchcock adds this thought: "Here is the astounding part. *Dubai Internet City was designed, built, and made available to tenants in only twelve months.*"[25]

Expanding on what Saddam Hussein has already established in Babylon, from a biblical perspective, is inevitable. The capacity to create a significant city with Baghdad in its distant suburbs is within the reach of modern planners and builders. That it could happen quickly is certainly within the realm of possibility. All that is needed is for someone to say, "Let's do it!"

ON WHOSE AUTHORITY?

Having talked about the Bible's prediction that Babylon on the Euphrates will one day take its place again among the major cities of the world, a final question emerges with regard to who will have the authority in the Persian Gulf region to set this plan in motion. It may surprise you to learn that the Bible points the finger at Europe in cooperation with the Arab world. If so, where is the United States in all of this? The Bible doesn't answer that question directly, but it does imply more about America's role in end-time events than you may realize. Let's turn the page and think about that for a moment.

Chapter Ten

SETTING THE STAGE
The Role of Nations in Babylon's Future

The Roland surface-to-air missile seemed to come out of nowhere as it slammed into the back of Air Force Major Jim Ewald's A-10 Thunderbolt jet. It was April 8, 2003 and Major Ewald had just flown an assault mission over Baghdad. Suddenly he was in serious trouble as he struggled to maneuver his wounded aircraft to a safe landing area. He never made it.

As the A-10 floundered in the sky, it soon became obvious to Ewald that he would have to eject from the aircraft. Parachuting to the ground, he watched the $13 million jet plow into the Iraqi desert in a ball of fire. Ewald had survived but the plane was destroyed.

This is how Bill Gertz, the acclaimed defense and national security reporter for the *Washington Times* introduces his "bone-chilling exposé,"[1] *Treachery: How America's Friends and Foes are Secretly Arming our Enemies.* Gertz's point in telling Ewald's story is that the Roland missile that almost killed one of our American pilots and destroyed a $13 million American military investment was a French missile.

Indeed, the missile that shot down Ewald's A-10 was just one of many French weapons the Iraqis used against U.S. forces during—and after—the Iraq war. Only a week after Ewald's crash, a U.S. Army team searching Iraqi weapons depots at Baghdad International Airport discovered caches of French-made missiles. In one cache the team found fifty-one Roland-2 antiaircraft missiles, which had been produced through a partnership of French and German arms manufacturers. One missile bore the label "05-11 knd 2002," indicating that the batch had been produced just months earlier.[2]

Later, in a chapter titled "The French Connection," Gertz summarized his findings on France's covert and treacherous activities with Iraq.

The signs of France's corrupt dealings with Iraq were everywhere. In fact, according to a senior member of Congress who declined to be identified by name, by 2000 France was Iraq's largest supplier of military and dual-use equipment.[3]

France was not alone in these clandestine agreements with the enemy, of course. As we now know, Germany, Russia, and China were all supplying technology and equipment to Iraq behind the coalition forces' back. Bill Gertz labeled this action "Treachery," and from the U.S. perspective it was indeed just that.

The interesting point for me, however, is how far certain European countries were willing to go to court the favor of Saddam Hussein's Iraq. A combination of anti-American sentiment and greed led nations that were once U.S. allies to sleep with the enemy and put American lives at risk.

Yet money and resentment alone could not account for such treachery among friends. Both France and Germany had been courting Iraq for her energy resources and were highly motivated by oil contracts with Saddam in exchange for their willingness to supply him with his coveted military needs. In fact, "classified intelligence reports based on sensitive information revealed that Russia, along with France, secretly attempted to conclude lucrative oil deals with the Iraqi government in the days before U.S. military operations began."[4]

There is no question about it—Europe is passionate about Iraq. Britain is in Iraq with the coalition forces, and the France-Germany connection with Saddam is well documented. Other European nations are also involved in one way or another, contributing to the realization that

Iraq is a big deal for most of the EU. Whether openly, or by stealth or treachery, they're all there. Europe definitely wants a piece of the action in the future of Iraq.

LIKE A BEAR TO HONEY

Greece

Actually, Europe has been interested in Iraq for a long time—over 2300 years, to be exact. When Alexander the Macedonian defeated Darius the Persian at Gaugameles, and rode triumphantly into Babylon in 331 BC, he ignited the passion of Europe for the land of Mesopotamia. That passion was demonstrated by the fact that . . .

> Fourteen thousand Macedonians and an equal number of Babylonian women were married in what is still probably the largest mass wedding the world has ever known. By this grandiose gesture, Alexander intended to spread the message of...the union of Mediterranean and Middle Eastern peoples.[5]

Somewhere in Iraq, European blood still flows in Iraqi veins.

The Greek Seleucids continued to rule in Babylon after the death of Alexander the Great and perpetuated the Greek influence. This influence flowed in both directions, however, as "the borrowing of Babylonian culture by the Greeks brought many Babylonian ideas and inventions to Rome, and eventually to all of Europe."[6]

Rome

Rome had an equal interest in Babylon but was rebuffed by the Parthians of northern Persia who had established their control over the region after the Seleucids. Numerous attempts to extend the borders of the Roman Empire east into Mesopotamia met with repeated failure. As Munier observed, "from their Syrian outposts, the Romans dreamed of restoring Alexander's Eastern Empire."[7] In fact, though, due to the Muslim conquest of the entire area, which led to the Ottoman Empire and

Turkish rule, it would be centuries before Europe would once again insert itself into the Middle East.

Great Britain

Great Britain would be the next European nation to leave its fingerprint on the region. Having established a trading post for the East India Company in Basra during the 17th Century, Britain's involvement in Mesopotamia grew until the late 19th Century when the old European passion was reignited. In 1892 Lord Curzon, Viceroy of India, was quoted as saying, "It is thus imperative for the Crown to annex the area as a zone of absolute British influence."[8]

Following the discovery of oil, English involvement in Mesopotamia began to be challenged by the Germans. Kaiser Wilhelm II made a bid for a Berlin to Baghdad railway extending all the way to Basra, and courted the favor of the Turks and tribal chieftains to accomplish his purpose. With the advent of World War I, however, Britain quickly invaded Iraq and eventually expelled both the Turks and the Germans. Thus, at the beginning of the 20th Century, two European nations (England and Germany) were fighting over the destiny of Iraq.

After the British occupation and mandate leading up to the establishing of the sovereign state of Iraq in 1921, England continued to exercise a measure of control and influence over the fledgling nation. In fact, during World War II, the English occupied Iraq once again, but withdrew as the war ended. Then, anti-colonialism led to nationalism and the Pan-Arabism of Saddam Hussein's Ba'ath party, and Great Britain was out. European nations no longer controlled Iraq, but that didn't mean that Europe was no longer interested in the region.

As the two Gulf Wars drew the world's attention back to Iraq, Europe was once again embroiled in Iraqi affairs. The British were there as a co-belligerent with the U.S.- led coalition, along with numerous other European nations. After reviewing the history of England's involvement in Iraq, we can perhaps better understand the willingness of the British to step back in as a force to clean up Saddam Hussein's mess.

France & Germany

France and Germany, on the other hand, had a much different history with Iraq. France's initial interest in Iraq had been trumped by England's dominant influence in the aftermath of World War I. The Germans had been defeated twice by the British in Iraq, losing both World Wars. Both of these nations stood on the outside looking in, and their limited participation in the first Gulf War left them in the same position of disadvantage. So, what did they do?

The French and the Germans (along with the Russians and the Chinese) sought to make private deals with Saddam Hussein in defiance of the sanctions imposed by the United Nations. Their strategy was to make money and establish favors that would position them for future access to Iraq's oil. The fact that they were doing business illegally and undermining the efforts of the rest of the world was obviously not a deterrent. Unadulterated greed drove them to treacherous betrayal. Acting without national integrity, they risked their reputation on Saddam's apparent ability to survive— and they lost. Now they are playing catch-up behind the United States and British post-war efforts.

What I am endeavoring to demonstrate is that Europe has had a long and vital interest in the territory we now know as Iraq. Whether it be the early Greeks and Romans, or the more contemporary Brits, Germans, and French, the land of Two Rivers has been a strategic part of Europe's global dreams. Iraq's strategic location in the Middle East, as well as its rich energy resources, has lured the European imperialists like a bear drawn to honey.

FEET OF IRON AND CLAY

So, what is so significant about Europe's involvement in Iraq? Well, prophetically speaking, that is exactly what God predicted would happen.

Those who are familiar with Daniel's prophecy of end-time events have been tracking the post-war developments in Europe toward unification knowing that this was the biblical expectation. Now as Europe is showing such an obvious bias toward the Arab world, even with a willingness to alienate former friends, including Israel, the picture is becoming even clearer. A revived Europe in concert with the Arab nations is what Daniel is apparently suggesting as the final empire of the Times of the Gentiles.

In chapter two of Daniel's prophecy, Nebuchadnezzar, king of Babylon, had a dream in which a huge metallic monster first appeared and then was decimated by an equally huge stone that struck the image on its feet. Very disturbed by this dream, the king challenged his wisest counselors to interpret the meaning of the nightmare.

He devised a crafty plan, however, that would insure the integrity of the counselors' interpretation, for they not only had to figure out the meaning, they also had to tell the king what he had dreamed. The wise men must have been dumbfounded. They could always come up with an interpretation of a dream—but how could they know what the king had dreamed if he didn't tell them?

Unlike the native Babylonian wise men, however, Daniel had an audience with God. Because of this, he was able to learn both the dream and its interpretation. Now, the point of this narrative as an introduction to the prophecy is to demonstrate that the whole thing was orchestrated by God. This incredible prediction of the succession of empires in the Middle East is so phenomenal that God devised an impossible scenario to convince the reader that the dream, and its interpretation, was truly of God. As they say today, this prophecy is a *God-thing*—a supernatural feat of divine foreknowledge.

In hindsight of history we can see that God was precise and accurate in His prediction as the succession of empires flowed from the Babylonians to the Persians to the Greeks, and finally to the Romans. Then, as we saw in an earlier chapter of this book, everything went dormant—until the new awakening in the 20th Century. Now, as we observe what is happening in Europe, Bible students are asking, *Could this be the fulfillment of the final element of Daniel's prophecy?* Let's think about that for a moment.

Daniel's Prophecy

First, let's read this part of Daniel's prophecy so we can get it fixed in our minds (Daniel 2:40-43).

40 And there shall be a fourth kingdom, strong as iron, because iron breaks to pieces and shatters all things. And like iron that crushes, it shall break and crush all these.

41 And as you saw the feet and toes, partly of potter's clay and partly of iron, it shall be a divided kingdom, but some of the firmness of iron shall be in it, just as you saw iron mixed with the soft clay.

42 And as the toes of the feet were partly of iron and partly clay, so the kingdom shall be partly strong and partly brittle.

43 As you saw the iron mixed with soft clay, so they will mix with one another in marriage, but they will not hold together, just as iron does not mix with clay.

The significant fact to notice as we begin to probe this aspect of Daniel's prophecy is that the toes and feet of the great image are symbolic references to the final kingdom of the Times of the Gentiles. This is indicated by the next verse (44) which states, "And in the days of those kings the God of heaven will set up a kingdom that shall never be destroyed." A "stone" (v. 34-35) in the prophecy represents this kingdom of Christ and we are told that the stone "struck the image on its feet of iron and clay, and broke them in pieces" (v. 34).

Here's the point: When Christ returns to set up His Kingdom on the earth, the empire He defeats will be the feet and toes portion of the image. So, if we can figure out who the feet and toes of iron and clay are, we will know who the end-time power in the Middle East will be.

The First Clue

Our first clue is that the major component of the feet and toes is iron. "It shall be a divided kingdom, but some of the firmness of iron shall be in it" (v. 41). Now, this is the same element as the legs which were the fourth kingdom of the ancient world. Bible scholars are agreed that the fourth empire of Daniel's vision is the Roman Empire. Iron is a fitting picture of the Romans in that they were like iron that "breaks to pieces and shatters all things" (v. 40). And since Daniel's prophecy is consistent in its use of the metallic symbols, that means that the strong component of the feet and toes will be a revival of "iron"—or, some form of the European power, represented in ancient times by the Roman Empire.

Europe is indeed reviving as a united power to the point where it is beginning to leverage its influence in Middle East affairs. If we are approaching the end of the Times of the Gentiles, as many Bible students believe, then the emergence of Europe as a significant force in the world is truly noteworthy.

The Second Clue

But the prophecy of Daniel indicates that the iron of the feet and toes will be "mixed with the soft clay" (v. 41). Now, many suggestions have been offered over the years as to the identity of the clay. Actually, the Aramaic word for "clay" is not the word for soft, raw clay, but refers to a "formed pottery object,"[9] like tile. In contrast to iron, tile is weak and brittle. This realization led the renowned prophetic scholar Dr. John F. Walvoord to say, "The intrusion of tile in an essentially metal construction, while perhaps decorative, has the symbolic meaning of weakness."[10]

One major difference between iron and clay is in its cohesive strength. Daniel makes this distinction. "And as the toes of the feet were partly iron and partly clay, so the kingdom shall be partly strong and partly brittle" (v. 42). In other words, the iron part of this empire will have a united strength, but the clay part will be a weak mixture of nations with very little cohesive togetherness.

Furthermore, this arrangement between iron and clay will not be a true union, but each will remain distinct from the other—"it shall be a divided kingdom" (v. 41). As with Alexander's army and the women of Mesopotamia, "they will mix with one another in marriage, but they will not hold together, just as iron does not mix with clay" (v. 43). It appears that Daniel is saying that these two entities will work at getting along together for a common purpose, yet they will remain separate powers and will not become truly united.

Now, as we look at the current situation around the Mediterranean Rim (the area of the Old Roman Empire), it is interesting to notice that it is shared by two major groups which have a striking resemblance to iron and clay. Europe is north of the sea and is fast becoming a strong united economic power reminiscent of iron. South and East are the Arab states of North Africa and the Middle East, currently united in a weak alliance known as the Arab League, which is very much like a brittle mosaic.

Together the areas inhabited by the Arab world and the European community form the Old Roman Empire of the Caesars.

So, the question arises, *Could a cooperative effort between these two very different groups be the final kingdom of the Times of the Gentiles predicted by Daniel?* The strength of a united Europe aligned with a more brittle partner in the Arab League seems to fit the biblical scenario.

THE PROPHECY PUZZLE

Identifying the contemporary fulfillment of the component parts of an ancient prophecy can be a tricky business. The gurus of prophetic interpretation often jump to premature conclusions in their rush to capture popular notice. History has taught us, however, that they are often wrong. Back in the early 1940s many were sure that Hitler was the Antichrist, and in the late 60s when Israel captured all of Jerusalem in the Six Day War, a whole host of prophecy watchers were certain that the end of the age was imminent. As we look back, we shake our heads and say, "Well, not exactly."

Recognizing true prophetic fulfillment is a lot like working a picture puzzle. As we continually compare our progress with the picture on the box, so careful interpreters continually compare what they see with the picture in the Bible. Some pieces look like they fit (the configuration is similar and the colors are a close match), but all of the elements are not quite there. If we try to force those pieces, we ruin the puzzle—as forcing inaccurate prophetic interpretations has ruined the confidence of many in the validity of biblical prophecy. If we are thoughtful and careful, though, we put those pieces back in the mix and continue to look for the piece that truly fits. Conscientious prophecy students do the same.

So, does this interpretation of the feet and toes of iron and clay in Daniel's prophecy truly fit the prophetic intention? Well, as a puzzle nears completion, it becomes easier to identify the remaining pieces. In like manner, as the full picture of end-time prophecy begins to emerge, the apparent complexity of certain prophetic pieces becomes clear.

Looking closely at the details is how we determine whether or not the interpretation truly fits the prophecy. So, let's do that. Let's examine the development of the European Union and the Arab League, as well as their affinity for each other to see if this part of the prophetic puzzle fits—and to observe how all of this affects the future of Iraq.

Chapter Eleven

UNLIKELY PARTNERS
Europe and the Arab World Working Together

Islamic terrorists are targeting Europe—not just the United States. There is a fundamental difference, though. The countries of Europe are the Arabs' neighbors. That makes them more accessible to terrorist activity, and therefore more vulnerable.

The Europeans obviously know that. They also know that Muslim immigration into their countries has threatened to change the demographics of their societies. The gradual Islamification of Spain is a prime example. In a world of shrinking independence, Europe must contend with the reality that it is merely a part of the Mediterranean community. North Africa and the Middle East are also part of their local world.

It is in the best interest of the Europeans therefore to develop a cooperative relationship with the Arab League. The two may not see eye-to-eye, but getting along is of paramount importance. Without question, Europe is pro-Arab—not pro-Israel. There is good reason for that.

So, what does all of this mean for Iraq? And, is this really what Daniel was predicting in his "feet and toes of iron and clay" prophecy?

THE STRENGTH OF IRON

"The logistics alone are incredible, the cost, the . . . everything."

"What?"

"He wants to move the U.N."

"Move it?"

Steve nodded.

"Where?"

"It sounds stupid."

"Everything sounds stupid these days," Bailey said.

"He wants to move it to Babylon."

"You're not serious!"

"*He* is."

"I hear they've been renovating that city for years. Millions of dollars invested in making it, what, New Babylon?"

"Billions."[1]

In the best-selling *Left Behind* series, LaHaye and Jenkins envision a powerful ruler coming out of Romania to lead the European Union. His name is Nicolae Carpathia, a gifted and charismatic personality who beguiles the nations into giving him absolute authority. Nicolae is the biblical Antichrist who sets his sights on a rebuilt Babylon in Iraq as the new headquarters of the United Nations.

Responding to this character and plot development in the *Left Behind* series Mark Hitchcock says,

> While the Left Behind series is fictional, it is based on God's blueprint for the end times in the Bible. And the rebuilding of New Babylon as the Antichrist's commercial, political headquarters is anything but a fable.[2]

LaHaye and Jenkins concur that a European leader will be interested in Babylon as the center of his operations. Their view is based upon a study of biblical prophecy and is being confirmed by modern developments in Europe.

The Ascendancy of Europe

Europe has emerged out of the ashes of World War II to become what some are touting as the most significant economic power in the world. The United States, of course, is still a major player in world affairs, but according to some the tide is turning. Europe is ascending and the U.S. is declining.

T.R. Reid, the former London bureau chief for the *Washington Post*, has written a celebrated book, *The United States of Europe: The New Superpower and the End of American Supremacy*, in which he says,

> At the dawn of the twenty-first century, a geopolitical revolution of historic dimensions is under way across the Atlantic: the unification of Europe. Twenty-five nations have joined together—with another dozen or so on the waiting list—to build a common economy, government, and culture. Europe is a more integrated place today than at any time since the Roman Empire. …The new United States of Europe—to use Winston Churchill's phrase—has more people, more wealth, and more trade than the United States of America.[3]

America is a nation of military power, but is declining in economic strength. Europe is a nation of military dependence, but is becoming an economic giant. Due to the military presence of America in NATO, Europe has been able to concentrate on economic rebuilding and has been free from military concerns. The United States, on the other hand, has assumed the position of policing the world against rogue states and has been forced to direct much of its national budget into military preparedness. The American economy unfortunately has taken a back seat.

The problem with this scenario is that economics is driving the global agenda, and the use of military force is increasingly demeaned as an antiquated approach to change. In that exchange, Europe is coming out on top and the United States has become the scapegoat of international criticism. Power is out and the utopian dream of economic paradise is in.

> When the United States was weak, it practiced the strategies of indirection, the strategies of weakness; now that the United States is powerful, it behaves as powerful nations do. When the European great powers were strong, they believed in strength and martial glory. Now they see the world through the eyes of weaker powers. These very

different points of view have naturally produced differing strategic judgments, differing assessments of threats and of the proper means of addressing them, different calculations of interest, and differing perspectives on the value and meaning of international law and international institutions.[4]

This quote from Robert Kagan in his book, *Of Paradise and Power*, illustrates the shift that has taken place and is propelling Europe into world ascendancy. I am often asked, "Is the United States mentioned in biblical prophecy as a major player in end-time events?" Well, apart from spiritualizing the text and making it say things other than what it actually says, the answer is, no! Daniel's prophecy emphasizes Europe as the dominant force at the end of the Times of the Gentiles. We are beginning to see the changes that will make that a reality.

1. Emergence of the European Union

The uniting of Europe seems to be proceeding more slowly than anticipated, but is nevertheless on track. It began on January 1, 1958 with six nations (Belgium, France, West Germany, Italy, Luxembourg, and the Netherlands) uniting in a European Economic Community. The union eventually grew to nine nations in 1973 (adding Denmark, Ireland and the United Kingdom) and then ten nations in 1981 (adding Greece). At that point prophecy gurus experienced an adrenaline high as they were sure the ten toes of Daniel's prophecy were then complete and in place. To their chagrin, however, Portugal and Spain were included in 1986 and nine years later (1995) Austria, Finland and Sweden brought the member states to fifteen. Then recently (May, 2004) ten additional nations were admitted (Cyprus, Czech Republic, Estonia, Hungary, Latvia, Lithuania, Malta, Poland, Slovakia and Slovenia), making the union twenty-five nations strong. Bulgaria and Romania gained acceptance in 2007 and Turkey is anxiously waiting in the wings. Other member states are being considered also, with the potential of increasing the strength of the union even more.

It is evident that we are just beginning to see the impact of what Europe is becoming. Already it is exceeding the United States in population, land mass and gross domestic product. According to one source "If considered a single unit, the European Union has the largest economy in the world with a 2004 GDP of 11,723,816 PPPs" (Purchase Power Parity).[5]

With a common currency, the euro, which "ranks as the world's strongest currency,"[6] the nations of Europe are now committed to an irreversible union. Member states have agreed to the text of a new constitutional treatise which is on track to become the first official constitution of the EU. In fact, "The New Europe has all the symbolic apparatus of a unified political entity."[7]

2. Comparison to the Old Roman Empire

In all of this there has been an interesting comparison made by many to the Old Roman Empire. The EU actually began with the Treaty of Rome in 1957, and although the union's activities have centered in Brussels, Strasbourg, and Luxembourg, the concept of a reunited Europe was conceived in the womb of Rome. Comparisons with the Old Roman Empire are therefore inevitable.

> Europe is a more integrated place today than at any time *since the Roman Empire* (emphasis added).[8]

> The new agreement to add ten new members is being called Europe's "biggest political union *since the Roman Empire*..." (emphasis added).[9]

> "For the first time *since the Roman Empire*, a large portion of Europe now shares a common currency" (CNN report - emphasis added).[10]

Two important things should be noticed in all of this with regard to our study. First, Europe is definitely back as a united entity and is fast becoming the most significant power in the world. Second, the EU has a cohesive strength that could easily be characterized as "iron-like." The Europeans are creating a massive political and commercial strength with a unified central control that is surpassing the United States as the real global superpower.

So, the Roman Empire has arisen out of the dust of antiquity—at least, the northern portion of the empire. Like so many of the Middle East nations, including Israel, the power of Rome is asserting itself again. But, what of the southern half of the empire in North Africa and the Middle East? Has that emerged as well? Well, yes—but not as iron. It has materialized as a tile mosaic.

BRITTLE AS CLAY

As the European nations have moved toward a cooperative union, so have the Arab states. In fact, the Arabs began moving toward a unified effort before Europe did. Twelve years before the charter of Rome (1957), which launched the European Economic Community, a league of Arab states was initiated in Cairo, Egypt. On March 22, 1945, seven Arab-speaking countries (Egypt, Iraq, Lebanon, Saudi Arabia, Syria, Transjordan, and North Yemen) signed a charter of alliance that has grown over the last sixty years to encompass twenty-two Arab nations. Today it is simply known as the Arab League.

Development of the Arab League

Formation of the Arab League actually proceeded in a similar pattern to the development of the European Union. Each began with a few nations agreeing to cooperate on a limited level for a common purpose and each grew in incremental levels as other nations decided over time to join the alliance. Slowly, separately, but steadily, both the Arabs and the Europeans engaged in unifying processes that have resulted in significant alliances on both sides of the Mediterranean Sea.

Egypt and six Middle East nations signed the first declaration of Arab unity in 1945. Three years later this League declared war on the newly created country of Israel—and lost. Such a humiliating defeat only raised the awareness in the Arab world that Arab unity was essential to the success of the Arab states.

African Arab nations soon joined the alliance in the 50s—Libya (1953), Sudan (1956), and Morocco and Tunisia (1958). It was at this point that the United Nations officially recognized the Arab League as "the UN's organization for education, science and culture in the Arab region."[11] Then other nations began to jump on the bandwagon—Kuwait (1961), Algeria (1962), South Yemen (1967), Oman, Qatar, the United Arab Emirates, and Bahrain (1971). In 1964 the Arab League recognized the formation of the Palestine Liberation Organization and, although the PLO did not have nation status, actually admitted them to the League in 1976.

So, as you can see, the Arab world has been developing a common alliance during the same period of time that the European community has been pursuing its unified system. Yet, there is a significant difference between the two as reflected in the nature of their unions.

A Brittle Alliance Like Tile

The European Union is a true union with individual nations surrendering their sovereignty to the common good of the collective group. It is an iron-clad alliance that is becoming increasingly strong now that they have a common currency and are pursuing a common constitution. This is not the case with the Arab League, however. In fact, the alliance of twenty-two Arab states cannot even be called a union because no supreme unifying authority exists.

For instance, in the initial formulation of the Arab League, Nuri al-Sa'id was the voice of Iraq in the negotiations. He had been resisting a radical pan-Arabism in the politics of Iraq and was dubious of Egypt's attempt to draw the Arab countries into a cooperative arrangement. Yet, "The charter of the League which emerged was . . . very much to Nuri's liking, since it enshrined the principle of the independent sovereignty of the member states and made only rhetorical reference to pan-Arabism."[12]

Actually the Arab League is "a voluntary association of independent countries"[13] where each country retains its sovereign status. The Arab League website makes the following admission:

> Egypt and some of the other Arab States wanted closer cooperation without the loss of self-rule that would result from total union. The original charter of the Arab League

created a regional organization of sovereign states that was neither a union nor a federation.[14]

The Arab League, then, is more like decorative tile than a strong iron edifice. The alliance looks good and serves a cosmetic purpose, but it is not likely to sustain the pressures of adversity. There is no common currency in support of a strong economic agenda and the League has no intention of working toward a unifying constitution. The objective is cooperation, not unification. Everything about the League of Arab States fits the biblical metaphor of a clay object, like ceramic tile. There is a cohesive togetherness, which has a pleasant appearance, but in comparison to Europe, the Arab League is more brittle than strong.

EURABIA EMERGES

According to Daniel's prophecy the iron and the clay will adhere together to form the final kingdom of Nebuchadnezzar's image. The feet and toes of this colossal figure, which are the iron and the clay, will be an extension of the legs of iron which we have seen to be the Empire of Ancient Rome. In other words, Daniel anticipates that there will be a revival of the Old Roman Empire, but not in the same form as it originally existed. It will be partly strong and partly brittle—as when tile is attached to an iron frame.

So the question arises, *could the European Union and the Arab League be the iron and clay combination that revives the Roman Empire at the end of the Times of the Gentiles?* Are we watching the feet and toes of the image appear before our very eyes? In my opinion, this appears to be exactly what we are seeing.

Consider the timing. The Arab League and the European Union began within a twelve-year span of each other, which in turn was coincident with the emergence of modern Israel and the other Middle East countries. That is not mere coincidence.

Also, consider the nature of each alliance. One is emerging strong as iron, and the other is developing as a weak clay-like vehicle for cooperation between independent sovereign states. This too is likely to be more than coincidental.

But a third consideration should certainly cause us to sit up and take notice. The EU and the AL are finding common ground in their hatred of Israel, which is mirrored in their consequent dislike for America. Europe is unabashedly pro-Arab, and anti-Semitism is growing once again in the European countries. Due to the large immigration of Islamic people into Europe with their persistent and coercive influence on European culture (a process the Arabs call "dhimmitude"), Europe is demonstrating an increasing sympathy for Arab causes. This growing affinity of Europe for the Arab world is drawing the two together in what Bat Ye'or, the Egyptian-born political analyst and historian, has called Eurabia.

> Europe, as reflected by the institutions of the EU, has abandoned resistance for dhimmitude, and independence for integration with the Islamic world of North Africa and the Middle East. The three most apparent symptoms of this fundamental change in European policy are officially sponsored anti-Americanism, antisemitism/anti-Zionism and "Palestinianism." These increasingly visible aspects of European policy are merely components of an overall vision for the transformation of Europe into a new geopolitical entity—Eurabia.[15]

As Ye'or indicates, one of the major influences fostering this Europe-Arab alliance is their mutual hatred of Israel. In a *Jerusalem Post* piece titled, "Europe's Arab Gambit," writer Caroline Glick begins the article by saying, "The poll conducted recently by the EU which found that Europeans consider Israel to be the single greatest threat to world peace shocked many and caused the EU's political leadership to cringe with embarrassment."[16] Later in the same article she exposed the nefarious beginnings of this official European "Israeli-phobia."

> In November 1973, French president George Pompidou and German chancellor Willy Brandt met in Paris and proclaimed a joint resolution aligning EC policy with the Arab demands against Israel. This, according to

Yeor was the first official European declaration of a unified foreign policy.[17]

This pro-Arab and Anti-Israeli policy in Europe is of particular interest to our study because it sets the stage for exactly what the Bible predicts concerning the geo-political and socio-religious climate at the end of the Times of the Gentiles. Consider the following:

• Europe and the Arab states are beginning to develop an alliance with great similarities to Daniel's prophecy of the feet of iron and clay. Together they represent the entirety of the Old Roman Empire. If this is true (and it certainly appears so) the stage is being set for final events leading to Armageddon.

• Europe is clearly the dominant partner, although Islamic terrorism is coercing many concessions from the Europeans. In keeping with this influential imbalance, I understand biblical prophecy to say that the Antichrist world-ruler will rise like a popular and powerful Caesar out of the iron portion of Eurabia. He will be a European, not an Arab. The economic and political conditions of the Mediterranean Rim are creating the atmosphere for such a man to emerge as the leader of the most powerful force of the 21st Century.

• Although initially protective of Israel for political reasons (probably for the purpose of ensuring the existence of a Palestinian state in both the Gaza Strip and the West Bank), the Antichrist and his system will eventually unleash a torrent of hatred against the Jewish state. The anti-Israel/anti-Semitic posture of the Arab world is already burning in the soul of the European Union. It is destined to erupt like a smoldering volcano—where there is smoke there will one day be fire.

All of which brings us back to our subject of the rebuilding of Babylon on the Euphrates River in Iraq. Europe, with its growing pro-Arab culture and politics, is becoming the most likely candidate for convincing Islamic leaders to cease their radical tactics of destruction—at least within the realm of Eurabia. As I mentioned in the previous chapter, when terrorism is eliminated the potential for a revived Babylon will be enormous.

Looking for a symbol of their togetherness, Europe and the Arab states will undoubtedly turn their attention once again to Babylon. With historic relevance, the significance of Babylon to both Europe and the Arab world is inescapable. It is a perfect place for the capital of Eurabia. Alexander the Great would applaud from his grave.

AN ABSURD THOUGHT? MAYBE

Why is America not in the biblical accounts of end-time prophecy? And why would the U.N. ever think of moving out of New York City to some other foreign destination—like Babylon? Well, maybe we should think "outside of the box" as it were, for both of these questions. Could it be that America or New York City will no longer exist? What is the possibility that Manhattan on the East River could cease being a suitable environment for the delegates of the world?

To grasp the significance of such thinking we need to put a few things into perspective. First, it is naïve to think that America is a Christian nation and therefore under the protective care of God. Liberal courts in conjunction with organizations like the ACLU have systematically eroded the Christian foundations of America. We are no longer what we once were—"one nation under God, with liberty and justice for all." As we have observed in the 2005 hearings for a new Supreme Court Justice, the issue of the killing of babies (abortion, i.e., Roe vs. Wade) is apparently the single most important criterion for becoming a Justice of the Supreme Court of the United States. As someone has said, "If God doesn't judge America, He will have to apologize to Sodom and Gomorrah."

Yet from a biblical point of view, America has most likely prospered above all other nations because it has been a safe haven for the Jewish people, and because it has been the sole protector of the nation of Israel.

God said to Abraham long ago, "I will bless those who bless you" (Gen. 12:3). America has blessed the Jewish people and God has blessed America beyond its wildest dreams.

A serious problem emerges in all of this, however. The blessings of affluence and power associated with support for Israel and the Jews have come with a price. All who identify with the Jewish state are hated by those who oppose it. America is hated by the Arab world, and increasingly so by the countries of Europe, for this very reason. Make no mistake about it—Eurabia is no friend of America.

As Europe capitulates to Arab demands and grows in its sympathy to the Muslim cause (through the process of dhimmitude),[18] it will be rewarded with decreasing Islamic terrorism and the assurance of peace. Consequently, Europe's anti-Americanism will become more prevalent and America will be increasingly isolated as the sole target of radical extremists.

WHAT IF?

So, what if the European Union turns a blind eye toward the plight of America and adopts a passive stance with regard to the U.S.-led resistance against terrorist activity? Remember—Germany, France, and Russia have already shown themselves as complicit in arming Iraq and other rogue states with weapons of mass destruction. And, as Bill Gertz clearly documents, rogue states have readily shared those same weapons and technology with terrorist organizations—including al Qaeda.

The question then arises, *What kind of situation could all of this produce?* Before describing the scary possibility of weapons of mass destruction in the hands of terrorists, Gertz puts forth a fictitious story that could very well become a prophetic reality.

The huge Saudi Arabian container ship arrived at the Red Hook Container Terminal in Brooklyn on a clear fall day. From the outside, the ship looked the same as the hundreds of other ships that docked at the terminal from Europe, Asia, and the Middle East. But the Saudi vessel was carrying a special cargo—one chosen with great care by Osama bin Laden, a Saudi national and the leader of the al Qaeda terrorist group that years before had attacked the World Trade Center, killing three thousand innocent men, women, and children. Hidden inside one of the ship's scores of blue metal shipping containers was a nuclear bomb. After years of trying, al Qaeda had succeeded in the difficult task of putting together a nuclear device, with help of Pakistani scientists, black market equipment purchases, and, finally, a quantity of plutonium purchased from Russian organized crime figures.

At the appointed hour, a blinding white flash signaled the detonation, followed by the explosion equal to the blast made by 10,000 tons of TNT. The shock wave spread in a large circle from the Brooklyn terminal, leveling almost everything in its path—from the Statue of Liberty in New York Harbor, to the buildings in the far north of Manhattan, to Kennedy Airport in Queens. The mushroom cloud could be seen as far away as Montauk Point, on the far tip of Long Island. Huge flames consumed everything that was left standing by the initial blast. The death toll from the immediate blast was staggering—at least 5 million people died instantly. Millions more died a slow, agonizing death from radiation sickness in the coming days.

Now, lest you should think that he is simply engaging in doomsday thinking, Gertz follows the above story with these remarks:

> The above scenario is fictional. But it is realistic. The truth is that terrorists are working on obtaining nuclear weapons of such destructive power that one detonation would have horrible consequences.
>
> Defense Secretary Donald Rumsfeld told me that he sees terrorists using weapons of mass destruction as the ultimate arms-proliferation threat. "Sure it worries me," Rumsfeld said. "It has to worry me. The lethality of those

kinds of capabilities is so substantial that one would be foolish not to be concerned and attentive."

The danger is real, and growing.[19]

Consider this disturbing thought. If Islamic extremists could nuke New York City as Gertz suggests, they would succeed in killing almost two million Jews—and that would be huge. You see, the terrorists are not just upset with America's riches and immorality, but all of Islam is out to get the Jews. That is one of the reasons that New York is a principal target of terrorist activity.

THINKING ABOUT THE POSSIBILITIES

So, is that the way it's going to happen? Well, not necessarily. But it would certainly explain why the U.N. would move to some other location. Yet, there are other reasons as well. Anti-Americanism could spread to the point where the United States could no longer tolerate the presence of international delegates from hostile countries. Or, maybe the rest of the world decides that America is not a fitting location for their deliberations. Or, how about the possibility that the Antichrist simply prefers Babylon as the identifying symbol of Eurabia and coerces the international body to do the same?

Whatever the reason, it does appear that the center of world activity will move to Babylon and Eurabia will be the force that makes it happen. How do we know that? The Bible seems to say so.

Chapter Twelve

THE END GAME
Armageddon and the Fall of Babylon

The biblical story begins in Iraq with the Garden of Eden, the fall of man, Noah's flood, and the great Tower of Babel. Then, with spiritual and cultural roots immersed in the land of Mesopotamia, the history of mankind returns time and again to this foundational site as the human story flows through the Bible. Whether Babylon or Nineveh, Shinar or Chaldea, these names of long ago dot the biblical landscape and focus our attention over and over on the land of black mud—what we now know as Iraq.

But the Bible also ends in Iraq. With a bang reminiscent of a nuclear explosion, Babylon in Iraq becomes the exclamation point of the finale of God's terminal judgment on the Gentile nations. In a crescendo of epic proportions, God challenges the day of man's ultimate exhibition of arrogant power and decimates the forces of evil.

You are probably familiar with the term Armageddon, right? Usually it appears as an apocalyptic reference to the end of the world where something like a nuclear holocaust annihilates humankind from the face of the earth. Well, according to the Bible, that's not exactly the way it will be.

Armageddon is a biblical word that is descriptive of events surrounding the end of the age and the termination of national powers as we know them. But it is not a reference to the end of the world.

The word for mountain in the Hebrew language is "har." On the western end of the expansive Jezreel Valley, which runs across the middle portion of northern Israel, sits the infamous mountain (or large hill) of

Megiddo. So, the Mountain of Megiddo in Hebrew is literally "har-megiddo"—or, as it comes down to us in English, "Armageddon."

The "Mountain of Megiddo" is a real place in northern Israel which guards the strategic pass of travel from the east and north into the western coastal area that leads south to Jerusalem and on to Egypt. Ancient armies traversing the Fertile Crescent had to maneuver through this pass around Megiddo, which made that particular mountain a strategic stronghold in Middle East wars.

After surveying the Jezreel Valley, which funnels into the Mountain of Megiddo, Napoleon said that Armageddon was "the most ideal battlefield he had ever seen."[1]

In fact, it seems that more wars have been fought in the region of Armageddon than in any other place in the world.

According to the Bible, then, this is the place where the war that will end all wars will commence. At the conclusion of the Armageddon campaign, the Bible describes Jesus Christ descending out of heaven as the Almighty King of kings who proceeds to destroy the combined military powers of the earth.

And coincident with this all-consuming military disaster is the divine judgment on Babylon—destroyed by an act of God like Sodom and Gomorrah. Fire will scream out of heaven with searing devastation and the grand symbol of man's power and authority perched as a tawdry harlot on the banks of the Euphrates River will be annihilated.

THE GREAT WAR

So, let's take a close look at the Battle of Armageddon. What does the Bible actually say about it? We read this account in the Book of Revelation, chapter 16.

> **12** The sixth angel poured out his bowl on the great river Euphrates, and its water was dried up, to prepare the way for the kings from the east.

13 And I saw, coming out of the mouth of the dragon and out of the mouth of the beast and out of the mouth of the false prophet, three unclean spirits like frogs.

14 For they are demonic spirits, performing signs, who go abroad to the kings of the whole world, to assemble them for the battle on the great day of God the Almighty.

15 ("Behold, I am coming like a thief! Blessed is the one who stays awake, keeping his garments on, that he may not go about naked and be seen exposed!")

16 And they assembled them at the place that in Hebrew is called Armageddon.

Notice that this war is called the war of "the great day of God the Almighty" (v. 14) and that it takes place at Armageddon (v. 16), the Mount of Megiddo. All other wars in the history of the world have been initiated by men, but Armageddon is God's war. God allows demonic spirits with magical powers (v. 14) to entice the kings of the earth into a showdown of power—a global rumble on the greatest battlefield of the world.

Now, why would they do that? And what makes the Jezreel Valley in northern Israel such a suitable place for the ultimate international crisis? Well, Jerusalem seems to be the prize, and if the hostile forces are coming from the east (v. 12) the best place to defend Jerusalem is at the Megiddo pass. It has always been that way.

Here's the apparent strategy for the defense of Jerusalem: Engage the enemy in the expansive valley flowing westward off the eastern slopes of Mount Megiddo and use the Megiddo pass as a fall-back position to funnel the enemy forces into a more constricted, less defensible position. If the enemy proves too strong, then retreat south to the Mountains of Judea leading up to Jerusalem and engage them there. As a last resort, fall back within the walls of Jerusalem as the ultimate defense.

This appears to be what happens in the Battle of Armageddon. It begins in the Jezreel Valley with Mount Megiddo as the focal point (Rev. 16:12-16). Then the whole scene flows south to Jerusalem where the kings of the earth are all gathered for the last throes of the Armageddon conflict

(Zech. 14:2). It is there that the King of kings, Jesus Christ, descends out of heaven and decimates the armies of the world (Rev. 19:11-21).

So, who's fighting whom? Well, remember that the Antichrist sets himself up to be worshiped as "God" in the temple of Israel in Jerusalem toward the end of the Times of the Gentiles (2 Thess. 2:4). The elimination of the state of Israel and an ethnic purge of the Jewish race has always been the goal of Eurabia, and the Antichrist seems to accomplish (Rev. 12:13-17) what Saddam Hussein could only dream about.

Now, we need to understand what the Bible is saying about this sequence of events. Apparently the security forces of the European Union will suddenly turn on the Jews and occupy their country. The Antichrist will then ride triumphantly into Jerusalem like the Roman conquerors before him and erect a statue of himself in the Holy Place of the Jewish Temple.

It is at this point that the Jews will scatter for fear of their lives (Matt. 24:15-21) as the Antichrist settles in to claim his prize. Because the EU security forces will have already become entrenched in the country as the protectors of Israel's borders, the takeover will be quick and effective. Jerusalem and the state of Israel will then belong to the Antichrist and the Arab League will applaud.

Such a move will undoubtedly put the oriental world on high alert. The Antichrist's arrogant betrayal of Israel, coupled with his egotistical claim to deity, will not settle well with the nations of the Pacific Rim that have never been part of the Eurabian alliance. China will no doubt have its own agenda for world dominance and will eventually challenge the Antichrist's boast of being the King of the World. With an army of two million (Rev. 9:16), the invaders from the East will cross the Euphrates basin to engage the forces of the West in the Valley of Jezreel at Armageddon.

The defenders of Jerusalem in the Battle of Armageddon, therefore, are the forces of the Antichrist and the aggressors are the kings of the East (Rev. 16:12). The Bible tells us that the kings of the east will be enticed by demonic influence (Rev. 16:14) to invade the kingdom of the Antichrist, evidently to expand their authority and power in the world. The Battle of Armageddon, therefore, will be the ultimate showdown between East and

West—World War III. How fitting that the whole Gentile world should be gathered around Jerusalem as the Times of the Gentiles comes to a close.

OUT OF THE BLUE

The prophets are clear that the Battle of Armageddon terminates in Jerusalem. True, according to John in the Book of Revelation it commences at the Mount of Megiddo, but Zechariah has Jesus descending on the Mount of Olives in Jerusalem as He encounters the armies of the world, not the Mount of Megiddo (Zechariah 14):

> **2** For I will gather all the nations against Jerusalem to battle, and the city shall be taken and the houses plundered and the women raped. Half of the city shall go out into exile, but the rest of the people shall not be cut off from the city.
>
> **3** Then the LORD will go out and fight against those nations as when he fights on a day of battle.
>
> **4** On that day his feet shall stand on the Mount of Olives that lies before Jerusalem on the east, and the Mount of Olives shall be split in two from east to west by a very wide valley, so that one half of the Mount shall move northward, and the other half southward.

You see, according to Zechariah, the culmination of the Armageddon conflict occurs in Jerusalem and, like the Assyrians and Babylonians and Romans of old, a siege of Jerusalem is the final stage of conquering the city. Now the kings of the East are the ones doing the sieging and the king of the West (the Antichrist) is the one who is besieged within the walls. They are all fighting one another until something totally unexpected happens. The heavens open and the Almighty Son of God begins His descent upon them. The time has come in the plan of God for the door of the Times of the Gentiles to be slammed shut (Rev. 19).

> **11** Then I saw heaven opened, and behold, a white horse! The one sitting on it is called Faithful and True, and in righteousness he judges and makes war.

12 His eyes are like a flame of fire, and on his head are many diadems, and he has a name written that no one knows but himself.

13 He is clothed in a robe dipped in blood, and the name by which he is called is The Word of God.

14 And the armies of heaven, arrayed in fine linen, white and pure, were following him on white horses.

15 From His mouth comes a sharp sword with which to strike down the nations, and he will rule them with a rod of iron. He will tread the winepress of the fury of the wrath of God the Almighty.

16 On his robe and on his thigh he has a name written, King of kings and Lord of lords.

17 Then I saw an angel standing in the sun, and with a loud voice he called to all the birds that fly directly overhead, "Come, gather for the great supper of God,

18 to eat the flesh of kings, the flesh of captains, the flesh of mighty men, the flesh of horses and their riders, and the flesh of all men, both free and slave, both small and great."

19 And I saw the beast and the kings of the earth with their armies gathered to make war against him who was sitting on the horse and against his army.

20 And the beast was captured, and with it the false prophet who in its presence had done the signs by which he deceived those who had received the mark of the beast and those who worshiped its image. These two were thrown alive into the lake of fire that burns with sulfur.

21 And the rest were slain by the sword that came from the mouth of him who was sitting on the horse, and all the birds were gorged with their flesh.

Such an exhibition of annihilating power is hard to conceive, and yet the devastating effect of Christ's Word surpasses the force of a nuclear event. The energy proceeding from His mouth levels the field and carrion birds are invited to a great feast of the dead.

This is not the end of the world, you understand. It is, however, the end of the time when Gentile nations rule in the realm of men and it is the beginning of the Kingdom of the Lord on earth. The trumpet and vial judgments of God spoken of earlier in Revelation will have purged the earth with fire and the Messiah-King will recreate the earth into its former Eden image when all things were beautiful and perfect.

So the Battle of Armageddon is the end of the old earth and heralds the beginning of the new earth in the Kingdom Age. That is the ultimate message of biblical prophecy.

BY FIRE AND BRIMSTONE

As the Battle of Armageddon climaxes in Jerusalem with Jesus Christ claiming His city of promise, the contrastive city of evil on the Euphrates River in Iraq is simultaneously obliterated from the face of the earth. On the heels of the Battle of Armageddon is the annihilation of Babylon. Notice the sequence in Revelation 16. After describing the development of the Armageddon conflict, the prophet John goes on to say:

> 17 The seventh angel poured out his bowl into the air, and a loud voice came out of the temple, from the throne, saying, "It is done!"
>
> 18 And there were flashes of lightning, rumblings, peals of thunder, and a great earthquake such as there had never been since man was on the earth, so great was that earthquake.
>
> 19 The great city was split into three parts, and the cities of the nations fell, and God remembered Babylon the great, to make her drain the cup of the wine of the fury of his wrath.
>
> 20 And every island fled away, and no mountains were to be found.

21 And great hailstones, about one hundred pounds each, fell from heaven on people; and they cursed God for the plague of the hail, because the plague was so severe.

As I mentioned before, the major argument for rebuilding the city of Babylon at the end of the age is that the old Babylon was never destroyed in the manner predicted by God. The prophet Isaiah was very specific in describing the ultimate demise of Babylon. He said that God (not men) would destroy Babylon, and that He would do it in the same way that He destroyed Sodom and Gomorrah—by fire out of heaven and a great earthquake (Isaiah 13):

> **6** Wail, for the day of the LORD is near;
> as destruction from the Almighty it will come!
> **7** Therefore all hands will be feeble,
> and every human heart will melt.
> **8** They will be dismayed;
> pangs and agony will seize them;
> they will be in anguish like a woman in labor.
> They will look aghast at one another;
> their faces will be aflame.
> **9** Behold, the day of the LORD comes,
> cruel, with wrath and fierce anger,
> to make the land a desolation
> and to destroy its sinners from it.

> **13** Therefore I will make the heavens tremble,
> and the earth will be shaken out of its place,
> at the wrath of the LORD of hosts
> in the day of his fierce anger.

> **19** And Babylon, the glory of kingdoms, the
> splendor and pomp of the Chaldeans, will be like
> Sodom and Gomorrah when God overthrew them.

Can you feel the panic and sense the fear?

It's a day like any other day in the city of opportunity and unlimited pleasure. People buying and selling, eating and drinking, lusting and indulging—and suddenly, without warning, the ground begins to tremble as the first bolt of lightning leaves its jagged image blazing across the darkened sky. Deafening thunder splits the air in repeated volleys as hail and fire begin to fall like volcanic boulders out of the sky.

Tremors become upheavals and cracking fissures turn into gaping wounds as beautiful buildings lose their balance and crumble into oblivion. Nothing is steady. There is no place to anchor hope.

The initial spray of laser pellets from above now becomes 100-pound fiery projectiles screaming out of the sky. Brimstone is hell in flight and the devastation is unimaginable: People pounded into the ground like ants swatted with hammers. Cars, busses and taxis crushed beyond recognition. Scrap metal plummeting into the abyss of an angry earth.

Fire engulfs the city as black, ugly smoke billows into the sky. Nothing stirs—anywhere. Twisted steel and broken concrete sprawl across the charred landscape and ashes are all that remain. No one survives—no one. Babylon is no more.

And it all happens in less than an hour—"For in a single hour your judgment has come" (Rev. 18:10; cf. 18:19).

HALLELUJAH

The word hallelujah means "praise the Lord," or literally, "praise Jehovah." It occurs only four times in the New Testament and "all four occurrences come in Revelation 19:1-6 in response to the destruction of the city of Babylon in Revelation 18."[2]

Revelation 19

1 After this I heard what seemed to be the loud voice
of a great multitude in heaven, crying out,

"Hallelujah! Salvation and glory and power belong to
our God,

2 for his judgments are true and just; for he has judged
the great prostitute who corrupted the earth with her

immorality, and has avenged on her the blood of his servants."

3 Once more they cried out, "Hallelujah! The smoke from her goes up forever and ever."

4 And the twenty-four elders and the four living creatures fell down and worshiped God who was seated on the throne saying, "Amen. Hallelujah!"

5 And from the throne came a voice saying, "Praise our God, all you his servants, you who fear him, small and great."

6 Then I heard what seemed to be the voice of a great multitude, like the roar of many waters and like the sound of mighty peals of thunder, crying out, "Hallelujah! For the Lord our God the Almighty, reigns."

This concluding outbreak of praise to the Lord is a reflection of joy that God has triumphed over evil. The destruction of Babylon has paved the way for the Kingdom of Christ to be established on the earth. It is the end of Satan's usurped reign over the affairs of men which he initiated in the Garden of Eden in the territory of Babylon. All that is bad is now gone and a new creation will introduce the future. Praise the Lord!

That is the conclusion of the story of Iraq as reflected in the Bible. All along, Babylon has been the focal point of Iraq's history. It is a saga that stretches from Babylon to Baghdad—and back again to Babylon.

But that is not the end—not the end of the world, nor the end of the story. The Kingdom of Christ will be the new era rising out of the ashes of Babylon. A new heaven and a new earth will be enjoyed by the people of God (Isaiah 65:17; 66:22) and righteousness will reign from the throne of Christ in Jerusalem. He is the Prince of Peace and "Of the increase of his government and of peace there will be no end" (Isaiah 9:7). All of creation shall return to its pristine state and life will be better than it has ever been since the day of Adam and Eve.

Yet, the Bible is clear that only believers in Christ will enter the Kingdom. Believing that He is the Son of God and that His death on the cross paid the penalty for our sin is the prerequisite for Kingdom-living (John 20:30-31).

Salvation from our sin according to the Bible is not in a church or creed, but is found only in the person of Jesus Christ (Acts 4:12). Salvation in the Bible is presented as a personal matter between us and Him (Acts 16:31). Our decision to repent of our sins and to receive Jesus Christ as our personal Savior is the crucial decision of our lives (John 1:12). The bottom line is that our sins must be forgiven before we can enjoy fellowship with Christ in His Kingdom.

Now the ball is in your court. The question is *How will you respond to Jesus Christ? Will you receive Him as your personal Savior and Lord of your life, or will you oppose Him in the tradition of Babylon?* Remember, the consequences are monumental.

This is the lesson of *Iraq: In the Crosshairs of Destiny.*

END NOTES

PRELUDE – In God's Time

[1] Gilles Munier, *Iraq: An Illustrated History and Guide,*(Northampton, Massachusetts: Interlink Publishing Group, Inc., 2004), p. 1.

CHAPTER ONE – Out of the Mud

[1] Daniel 2:1-16.
[2] Daniel 2:37.
[3] Daniel 2:20, 21.
[4] Daniel 2:37.
[5] Daniel 2 & 7.
[6] Revelation 16:12-16.
[7] Timeline of Iranian History, "Bridging East and West, 1851-1906" MAGE Publishers, 1999, www.mage.com/TLbody.html.
[8] Ibid., "1906."
[9] Ibid., "1935."
[10] Gilles Munier, *Iraq: An Illustrated History and Guide*, (Northampton, Massachusetts: Interlink Publishing Group. Inc., 2004), p. 2.
[11] Luke 21:24.
[12] Daniel 9:24-27.
[13] Daniel 9:25-26.
[14] Sir Robert Anderson, *The Coming Prince* (Grand Rapids, Michigan: Kregel Publications, 1957), pp. 72, 75. (Anderson clearly demonstrates that the biblical prophetic year is 360 days, instead of the Julian Calendar 365 days.)
[15] Daniel 9:27.
[16] Ibid.

CHAPTER TWO – Surprise! Surprise!

[1] Romans 9:17.
[2] Daniel 4.
[3] *Newsweek,* December 22, 2003, p. 23.
[4] Ibid., p. 27.
[5] Genesis 3.
[6] Psalm 2:4.

CHAPTER THREE - Babylon: The Eclipse of Eden

[1] *The Illustrated Bible Dictionary,* Vol. 1 (Wheaton, Illinois: Tyndale House Publishers, Inc., 1980), p. 409.
[2] Ibid., p. 408.
[3] Ibid., p. 409.
[4] Carl Roebuck, *The World of Ancient Times* (New York: Charles Scribner's Sons, 1966), p. 19.
[5] Alexander Hislop, *The Two Babylons,* 2nd Amer. Ed. (Neptune, New Jersey: Loizeaux Brothers, Inc., 1959), p. 25.
[6] Ibid., p. 22.
[7] Ibid., p. 12.
[8] Charles Dyer, with Angela E. Hunt, *The Rise of Babylon* (Wheaton, Illinois: Tyndale House Publishers, Inc. 1991), p. 60.
[9] Ibid., p. 65.

CHAPTER FOUR – The Empire that Was

[1] Jack Wheeler, "Unraveling Iraq's Real Agenda," *Orlando Sentinel*, October 28, 1990. Sec. G., p.1.
[2] Ibid.
[3] Ibid.
[4] Ibid., p. 6.
[5] Ibid.
[6] Ibid.
[7] Elaine Sciolino, *The Outlaw State: Saddam Hussein's Quest for Power and the Gulf Crisis* (New York: John Wiley & Sons, Inc., 1991), p. 218.
[8] Ibid., p. 220.
[9] Ibid., p. 218.
[10] Ibid., p. 215.
[11] Ibid., p. 214.
[12] Ibid., p. 223.
[13] Ibid., p. 200.
[14] "Rebuilding Babylon," *Christianity Today* (Carol Stream, Illinois), November 18, 1988, p. 71.
[15] Robert D. Culver, *Daniel and the Latter Days* (Chicago: Moody Press, 1954), p. 111.

CHAPTER FIVE – Ghost of Kuwait

[1] Elaine Sciolino, *The Outlaw State: Saddam Hussein's Quest for Power and the Gulf Crisis* (New York: John Wiley & Sons Inc., 1991), p. 220.
[2] Ibid., p. 30.

[3] Ibid., p. 191.

[4] Ibid., pp. 112-113.

[5] Ibid., p. 184.

[6] CARDRI, "Saddam's Iraq: Revolution or Reaction?" (Atlantic Highlands, New Jersey: Zed Books Ltd., 1989) p. 243.

[7] Sciolino, p. 187.

[8] Ibid., p. 188-189.

[9] George Rawlinson, as quoted by Hobart E. Freeman in his book, *Nahum, Zephaniah, Habakkuk – Minor Prophets of the Seventh Century B.C.*, (Chicago: Moody Press, 1973), p. 101.

CHAPTER SIX – Babylon: City of Destiny

[1] James Wellard, *Babylon* (New York: Saturday Review Press, 1972), p. 199.

[2] H. A. Ironside, Litt.D., *Expository Notes on the Prophet Isaiah* (Neptune, New Jersey: Loizeaux Brothers, 1975), pp. 85-86.

[3] Edward J. Young, *The Book of Isaiah,* Vol. I (Grand Rapids, Michigan: William B. Eerdmans Publishing Co., 1976), p. 427.

[4] Charles H. Dyer with Angela E. Hunt, *The Rise of Babylon* (Wheaton, Illinois: Tyndale House Publishers, Inc., 1991), p. 29.

[5] "Babylon's Glory Days are Reborn" – Associated Press, *Orlando Sentinel*, Sept., 1989.

[6] John Martin, "Isaiah," *The Bible Knowledge Commentary: Old Testament,* John F. Walvoord, Roy B. Zuck, ed. (Wheaton, Illinois: Victor Books, 1985), p. 1060.

[7] Ibid.

[8] Ibid.

[9] Charles Rollin, *The Ancient History of the Egyptians, Carthaginians, Assyrians, Babylonians, Medes and Persians, Macedonians and Grecians,* Vol. II (Philadelphia: J.B. Lippincott & Co., 1866), pp. 17-20.

[10] Ibid., p. 19.

[11] Ibid.

[12] Wellard, *Babylon*, p. 199.

[13] Dyer, *The Rise of Babylon*, pp. 26-27.

[14] Ibid., p. 162.

[15] Ibid., pp. 172-174.

CHAPTER SEVEN – Touchstone of Religion

[1] In a number of quotations throughout this chapter, bold type has been employed for emphasis by the author.

[2] Alexander Hislop, *The Two Babylons,* 2nd Amer. Ed. (Neptune, New Jersey: Loizeaux Brothers, Inc., 1959), p. 13.

[3] Ibid., p. 14.

[4] Ibid., pp. 20-21.

[5] Genesis 11.

[6] See *The Witness of the Stars* by Ethelbert W. Bullinger, D.D. (Kregel Publications, 1967), and *The Gospel in the Stars* by Joseph A. Seiss (Kregel Publications, 1972).

[7] Joseph A. Seiss, *The Gospel in the Stars* (Grand Rapids, Michigan: Kregel Publications, 1972), p. 15.

[8] Hislop, pp. 74-75.

[9] John Martin, "Isaiah," *The Bible Knowledge Commentary: Old Testament,* John F. Walvoord, Roy B. Zuck, ed. (Wheaton, Illinois: Victor Books, 1985), p.1061.

[10] Charles Rollin, *The Ancient History of the Egyptians, Carthaginians, Assyrians, Babylonians, Medes and Persians, Macedonians and Grecians,* Vol. III (Philadelphia: J.B. Lippincott & Co., 1866), p. 272.

[11] Ibid.

[12] Ibid., p. 274.

[13] Clarence Larkin, *The Book of Revelation* (Fox Chase, PA: Clarence Larkin, 1919), p. 161.

[14] Ibid.

CHAPTER EIGHT – Babylon Among the Nations

[1] Lt. Carey H. Cash, *A Table in the Presence* (Nashville, Tennessee: W Publishing Group, a Division of Thomas Nelson, Inc., 2004), p.181.

[2] Ibid., p. 229.

[3] Ibid., pp. 229-230.

[4] Rev. 17:5, KJV.

[5] Rev. 17:1, 15, KJV.

[6] Rev. 17:16, NAS.

[7] Mark Hitchcock, *The Second Coming of Babylon* (Sisters, Oregon: Multnomah Publishers, Inc., 2003), p. 99.

[8] Henry M. Morris, *The Revelation Record* (Wheaton, Illinois: Tyndale House Publishers, 1984), p. 355.

[9] John F. Walvoord, *The Revelation of Jesus Christ* (Chicago: Moody Press, 1966), p. 264.

[10] Charles H. Dyer with Angela Elwell Hunt, *The Rise of Babylon* (Wheaton, Illinois: Tyndale House Publishers, Inc., 1991), p. 30.

[11] *The Rise of Babylon* (published by Tyndale, 1991) and *What's Next?* (published by Moody Publishers, 2004).

[12] Dyer, *The Rise of Babylon*, pp. 19, 23.

[13] Hitchcock, p. 91.

[14] Morris, p. 349.

[15] Alexander Hislop, *The Two Babylons* (Neptune, New Jersey: Loizeaux Brothers, 1943), pp. 1-2, 91).

[16] Walvoord, p. 250.

[17] Dyer, *The Rise of Babylon,* p. 27.

[18] Elaine Sciolino, *The Outlaw State: Saddam Hussein's Quest for Power and the Gulf Crisis* (New York: John Wiley & Sons, Inc., 1991), pp. 191-192.
[19] Ibid., p. 192.

CHAPTER NINE – Not Exactly A Miracle

[1] Victor Davis Hanson, *Between War and Peace* (New York: Random House Trade Paperbacks, 2004), p. 33.
[2] Ibid., pp. 43-44.
[3] Amy Chua, *World on Fire: How Exporting Free Market Democracy Breeds Ethnic Hatred and Global Instability* (New York: Anchor Books, A Division of Random House, Inc., 2004), p. 198.
[4] Iraq Country Analysis Brief, June, 2005, "Iraq: Oil," www.eia.doe.gov/emeu/cabs/iraq.html.
[5] Mark Hitchcock, *The Second Coming of Babylon* (Sisters, Oregon: Multnomah Publishers, Inc., 2003), pp. 147-148.
[6] CNN Money, "Iraq's oil losses put at $11.4 billion," www.money.cnn.com/2005/07/04/news/international/iraq_lost.dj/.
[7] Iraq Country Analysis Brief, June, 2005, "Iraq: Exports," www.eia.doe.gov/emeu/cabs/iraq.html.
[8] Ibid., "Iraq: Oil."
[9] Howard LaFranchi, "Why Iraq oil money hasn't fueled rebuilding," July 14, 2005, www.csmonitor.com/2005/0714/p02s01-woiq.html.
[10] Ibid.
[11] Peter A. Clayton and Martin J. Price, *The Seven Wonders of the Ancient World* (New York: Routledge, 1988), Introduction.
[12] Clarence Larkin, *The Book of Revelation* (Fox Chase, Pennsylvania: Bethany Baptist Church, 1919), p. 161.
[13] L. Paul Bremer, III, Administrator, Coalition Provisional Authority, "Ministry of Agriculture Turnover, Baghdad," May 5, 2004, www.iraqcoalition.org/transcripts/20040505_bremer_ag.html.
[14] Nora Salim, "Iran prepares to ink oil deal with Iraq," *The Daily Star* (Lebanon), www.iht.com/getina/files/262223.html.
[15] Ibid.
[16] Salaam (Morning Daily), Tuesday, July 18, 1995, "Outstanding Issues in Iran-Iraq Relations," www.parstimes.com/history/outstanding_issues_iran-iraq.html.
[17] Ibid.
[18] Joseph J. Macielag, "The Twin Cities of the Tonawandas Welcomes You to the Western Terminus of the Erie Canal," www.the-tonawandas.com/canal.htm.
[19] Ibid.
[20] BBC News, Monday, 27 January, 2003, "Israeli tourism hits 20-year low," http://news.bbc.co.uk/1/hi/business/2697705.stm.
[21] BBC News, Friday, 24 December, 2004, "Iraq's tourism chief eyes the future," http://news.bbc.co.uk/2/hi/middle_east/4111369.stm.

[22] Ibid.
[23] Larkin, p. 162.
[24] Hitchcock, pp. 151-152.
[25] Ibid., p. 152.

CHAPTER TEN – Setting the Stage

[1] Greta Van Susteren, from back book jacket, *Treachery: How American's Friends and Foes are Secretly Arming our Enemies,* (New York: Crown Forum, 2004), written by Bill Gertz.
[2] Bill Gertz, *Treachery: How America's Friends and Foes are Secretly Arming our Enemies,* (New York: Crown Forum, 2004), p. 3.
[3] Ibid., p. 20.
[4] Ibid., p. 66.
[5] Gilles Munier, *Iraq: An Illustrated History and Guide,* (Northampton, Massachusetts: Interlink Publishing Group, Inc. 2004), p. 15.
[6] Ibid., p. 16.
[7] Ibid.
[8] Ibid., p. 29.
[9] John F. Walvoord, *Daniel: The Key to Prophetic Revelation* (Chicago: Moody Press, 1971), p. 69.
[10] Ibid., p. 70.

CHAPTER ELEVEN – Unlikely Partners

[1] Tim LaHaye and Jerry B. Jenkins, *Left Behind* (Wheaton, Illinois: Tyndale House Publishers, Inc., 1995), p. 352.
[2] Mark Hitchcock, *The Second Coming of Babylon* (Sisters, Oregon: Multnomah Publishers, 2003), p. 117.
[3] T.R. Reid, *The United States of Europe* (New York: Penguin Press, 2004) p. 1.
[4] Robert Kagan, *Of Paradise and Power* (New York: Vintage Books-A Division of Random House, Inc., 2003), pp. 10-11.
[5] *Wikipedia*, the free encyclopedia, "European Union," http://en.wikipedia.org/wiki/European_Union.
[6] Reid, p. 2.
[7] Ibid., p. 3.
[8] Ibid., p. 1.
[9] Hitchcock, p. 121.
[10] Ibid., p. 122.
[11] *Wikepedia*, "Timeline," http://en.wikipedia.org/wiki/Arab_League.
[12] Charles Tripp, *A History of Iraq*, 2nd Ed., (Cambridge: University Press, 2000), p. 119.
[13] Arab League Page, http://www.Arabji.com/ArabGovt/ArabLeague.htm.

[14] Ibid.

[15] Bat Ye'or, *Eurabia: The Euro-Arab Axis* (Madison, Teaneck: Fairleigh Dickinson University Press), p. 10.

[16] Caroline B. Glick, "Europe's Arab gambit," *The Jerusalem Post Upfront*, http://info.jpost.com/C003/Supplements/FSB/040102/art.06.html.

[17] Ibid.

[18] "The term dhimmitude comes from the Arabic word 'dhimmi.' It refers to subjugated, non-Muslim individuals or people that accept the restrictive and humiliating subordination to an ascendant Islamic power to avoid enslavement or death." (Taken from *Eurabia*, by Bat Ye'or, Preface.)

[19] Bill Gertz, *Treachery: How America's Friends and Foes are Secretly Arming our Enemies* (New York: Crown Forum, 2004), p. 205.

CHAPTER TWELVE – The End Game

[1] Mark Hitchcock, *The Second Coming of Babylon* (Sisters, Oregon: Multnomah Publishers, 2003), p. 136.

[2] Ibid., p. 139.

Dan Hayden is available for speaking engagements and personal appearances. For more information contact:

Dan Hayden
C/O Advantage Books
P.O. Box 160847
Altamonte Springs, Florida   32716

To purchase additional copies of this book or other books published by Advantage Books call our toll free order number at:
1-888-383-3110 (Book Orders Only)

or visit our bookstore website at:
www.advbookstore.com

Longwood, Florida, USA
"we bring dreams to life"™
www.advbooks.com

Printed in the United States
132892LV00004B/169-498/P